METROPOLITAIN
A PORTRAIT OF PARIS

MÉTROPOLITAIN

A PORTRAIT OF PARIS

**Matthew Weinreb
and Fiona Biddulph**

Phaidon Press Ltd
2 Kensington Square
London W8 5EP

First published 1994

©1994 Phaidon Press Limited
Photography © 1994 Matthew Weinreb

ISBN 0 7148 3156 5

A CIP catalogue record for this book is
available from the British Library.

Printed in Hong Kong

Acknowledgements
The author would like to thank all those who
have helped in the production of this book,
including the staff of the Bibliothèque
Historique de la Ville de Paris, the National
Art Library and the Conway Library. She would
also like to thank Lindy Spenser-Bernard,
Jenny Fraser, Nicholas and Siàn Biddulph,
and her husband, Anthony Fraser, for his help
and support.

Preceding pages
1 Military trophies adorn part of the Doric
frieze on the facade of the Dôme des Invalides,
designed by J Hardouin-Mansart for Louis XIV
in 1675.
2 Kisho Kurokawa's Japan Tower (1992), a
business centre and companion to
Spreckelsen's Grande Arche at La Défense.

Right: Statuary by Henri Bouchard from the
facade of the Neo-Byzantine-Romanesque
church, St-Pierre-de-Chaillot, designed
by Emile Bois. The church was built in 1937 to
replace the eighteenth-century parish church
in which Proust's funeral had been held in 1922.

Following pages
6 / 7 Decorative metal lattice-work on the
Eiffel Tower. Constructed by the engineer
Gustave Eiffel for the 1889 Universal
Exhibition, the tower is made up of 15,000
pieces of metal joined by 2,500,000 rivets.

Foreword

'Paris,' they said to me. 'We want you to do with
Paris what you did with London in *London
Architecture*.' Well, it was every photographer's
dream. Off I went!

As with the book on London, I was not concerned
with producing a categorical document of the city.
I wanted to wander, to walk with my eyes open (and
often upturned), to immerse myself in Paris's
repeating facades and grandeur and to spy-out the
details which are so often missed by the hurried
walker in the street.

I was immeasurably helped by the pride in which
every Parisian holds their city. Everybody has a
favourite corner or courtyard. I found many
intriguing spots simply because I was told, 'You
mustn't miss this.' I endeavoured not to.

Good architectural photography is dependent on
lighting: a ray of well-placed sunlight can make all
the difference between an exciting shot and a dull
one. Paris proved difficult in this respect. I shot in
September and October and, as the weather did not
favour me, many of the locations had to be visited
several times. Often this was an advantage since it led
to new perspectives on buildings and places and
meant that I saw (and was able to photograph) in a
different and unexpected way.

As always pre-planning was essential. The
Michelin atlas of Paris proved exceptionally good in
this respect, allowing me to determine the angles of
particular buildings and to select the best times to
shoot. Before I started I did not know Paris nearly as
well as I know London. I was, therefore, more than
usually dependent on other people's suggestions.
I would particularly like to thank Martin Meade in
this respect.

Paris is a city of great richness, both in its
architecture and in its self-image. It is well-maintained
and keeps its buildings to a human scale, while still
remaining sensuous and all-enveloping. It is rare to
feel overawed in Paris, except by the city's sheer
beauty. I hope that this book goes some way towards
conveying that feeling.

Matthew Weinreb, 1994

Neo-Rococo whirls into Art
Nouveau in the exuberant
gateway to Girault's Petit
Palais. The serpentine scrolls
of the Rococo style enjoyed a
revival in the closing years of
the nineteenth century and,
when the Petit Palais was
built in 1900, Art Nouveau
was at the peak of its
popularity.

Following pages
16/17 Stone Medusa's head
from the Palais de la
Découverte, the west wing of
Girault's Grand Palais. This
building was reopened as a
science museum for the 1937
Universal Exhibition.

9

Introduction

The final chapter of Ernest Hemingway's nostalgic Paris novel, *A Moveable Feast*, is called 'There Is Never Any End To Paris'. For me too, there is no limit to what the city has to offer. For centuries the wealth and talent of France has been poured into making Paris the cultural and political centre of Europe. The visual richness of the city is awe-inspiring. As you pace its streets and *quais*, your eyes drink in eight hundred years' worth of magnificently decorated buildings. The words *décor* and *décoration*, as well as *garniture*, are French and decoration is as essential to French architecture as garnish is to its food. As the historian Theodore Zeldin said, 'Puritanism and modesty are incompatible with whole-hearted gastronomy, which is unashamedly dedicated to the enjoyment of sensuality...' Parisians have a firm commitment to appearances and to the senses. Whether the display is in the window of the *pâtisserie* or on the facade of a building, its purpose is to delight the eye. It wasn't by accident that the painter Pierre Auguste Renoir called Charles Garnier's Opéra 'a lump of overcooked brioche'.

To get at the heart of Paris you have to peel away seemingly endless centuries of building, like the skins of an onion. Beginning with the sprawling suburbs and dormitory towns, the *Grands Ensembles* built up under de Gaulle in the 1960s, you travel round the *boulevard périphérique*, tracing the course of Thiers's mid-nineteenth-century fortifications, and down the arteries which lead into the core of the city, the island in the middle of the River Seine. It is here that everything began when a Gallic tribe, the Parisii, who fed themselves on the fish they caught in the river, founded a settlement over 2,000 years ago.

The city which began on the island has a different look for each season. In winter it can be grey and lowering, hunched under its Mansard roofs. In spring there is nothing so likely to lighten your step as the sunlight dancing off the Seine and through the first leaves on the trees along its banks. From about mid-July the island closes its shutters and bakes in the sun until the *Rentrée* at the beginning of September. Then you notice the countryside sneaking into the city. Convolvulus curls out of cracks in walls; grasses, lichens, mosses and ivies suddenly appear. And with the *Rentrée* comes the echo of a million impatiently tapping heels reverberating around the city. There are only four months to go before the *Sports d'Hiver*. Business must get done. Paris has both northern European and Latin sides to her character. Notre-Dame and the Sainte Chapelle are as Parisian as the Arc de Triomphe, but, while the first two are built in a northern European idiom, the latter is a version of a Roman building type.

The affair between Paris and Italy began in 53-2 BC, when Caesar's centurions took over the island in the middle of the Seine and named it Lutetia. They introduced their language, government, vineyards, temples and roads – some of which are still in use today. In 280 AD barbarians overran Lutetia and soon after the city was renamed Paris. Clovis, the king of the Franks, made the island his capital in 508 and took over the former palace of the Roman governors, on the site of the Palais de Justice.

Between the sixth and tenth centuries about 600 acres on the left and right banks of the Seine were developed, creating the first skin of the onion. During the reign of King Louis VI (1108-37), a wall was built to enclose and defend this area. A busy port was established on the *Grève*, or beach, now the place de l'Hôtel-de-Ville and in 1163 the foundation stone of Notre-Dame was laid. Soon after this Abélard and other teachers were given permission to cross over to the left bank and teach outside the cathedral's cloisters, a move which resulted in the founding of the Sorbonne in 1253.

In the years between 1180 and 1210 King Philippe Auguste built a new defensive wall around Paris, with the fortress of the Louvre at its western extremity. This wall was 10 feet thick and 20 feet high and parts of it can still be glimpsed today. On seeing it, Rabelais exclaimed, *'Par ma barbe, une vache avec un pet en abatroit plus de six brasses'* which translates roughly as 'By my beard, a cow could knock down six ells of it by breaking wind.' By the end of the fourteenth century King Charles V (1364-80) had enclosed another slab of the right bank with another wall, defended at the east end by the Bastille.

Many of the old fourteenth-century streets, such as the rue des Blancs-Manteaux and the rue des Hospitaliers St Gervais, are still there, despite the disappearance of the religious foundations after which they were originally named. The significance of others has long been forgotten, such as the rue des Ecouffes, which took its title from the Lombardian moneylenders (the rapacious 'kites'), and the rue des Mauvais-Garçons, which was the street of the hired assassins. The names of others have become corrupted over the years as they have been handed down by word of mouth. Impasse Putigneux, for example, was once the Rabelaisian-sounding impasse Pute Teigneux ('Scurvy Strumpet').

King François I (1515-47) was responsible for introducing the ideas of the Italian Renaissance to a Gothic city. Determined to rival the Italian courts in artistic excellence, he lured to France Leonardo da Vinci, Andrea del Sarto and Benvenuto Cellini, and commissioned the architect Pierre Lescot and the sculptor Jean Goujon to transform the Louvre into a Renaissance palace. Lescot's design was a revelation to the French and, although work had started on only two wings when he died, the new vocabulary of Classical forms which he used had already captured the French imagination.

The Religious Wars of the League raged during the greater part of the sixteenth century and they took their toll on Paris. Henri of Navarre, who was Protestant, laid siege to the city, which had been a stronghold of the Catholic League for five years. When he rode down from the heights of Montmartre and entered the city on 22 March 1594 he found a pitiful medieval settlement with its streets jammed with beggars and discharged soldiers. Determined to transform this chaos into the centrepiece of his new united kingdom, he embarked on the most revolutionary building programme in Europe.

The recognition that Paris is a beautiful city and the artist's desire to depict it first arose during the reign of King Henri IV. At the beginning of his reign topographical views of the city were rare. Yet, by the time of his assassination in 1610, he had inspired a generation of draughtsmen. It was Claude Chastillon's job to record the battles waged by the king's troops, but, setting out from his pied-à-terre in the new place Royale, he also began to draw the buildings of Paris and of other places throughout the realm. When he died, his meticulously observed drawings were engraved and published in 1641 in an edition called *Topographie Française*. By the mid-seventeenth century Paris led the field in the art of topographical print-making. Views by Silvestre, the Perelle family and the more romantic Jacques Callot were unsurpassed in Europe.

Meanwhile, Henri's successor King Louis XIII (1610-43) was enclosing another layer of land on the right bank to include the Louvre, on which work was being continued under Jacques Lemercier. With the construction of the new Jesuit church in the Marais, known as St-Paul-St-Louis, the latest Italian architectural style, the Baroque, was imported to Paris.

King Louis XIV (1643-1715), whose name was given to the most famous French style of all, used Paris as the setting for monuments to his own glory. In a famous memo of 1669 Colbert jotted down the king's ideas for the city: 'The Louvre to continue everywhere. Arches of Triumph for conquests of land. Observatory for the heavens. Pyramids...Grandeur and Magnificence.' King Louis replaced the city's fortifications on the right bank with leafy avenues – boulevards where Parisians promenaded and refreshed themselves at wayside cafés. Claude Perrault built his influential addition to the Louvre, a remarkable east-facing screen of 52 paired Corinthian columns and pilasters crowned by a massive pediment, and in 1664 Le Nôtre landscaped the tree-lined Jardin des Tuileries. The Sun King's patronage, masterminded by Colbert, stimulated an unprecedented flowering of the arts. Paris became a city dedicated to excellence in the manufacture of top-quality furnishings and the new Académie Royale d'Architecture sent its students to Rome to make accurate studies of Classical buildings.

After Louis XIV's death in 1715, the regent, Philippe Duc d'Orléans, moved the court back to Paris where it unwound from the strictures and formality of life at Versailles. It found a city bursting at the seams again, despite repeated outbreaks of cholera. Gasping for fresher air, the aristocracy moved into the new *hôtels particuliers* built by speculators along the faubourg St-Honoré and in the faubourg St-Germain. They decorated them lavishly in the frivolous new Rococo style, disseminated through the engravings of the Italian-born architect and designer Juste-Aurèle Meissonnier and through the designs of Gilles-Marie Oppenord. Among the new motifs were asymmetrical flowers and scrollwork, and rock and shell forms inspired by Italian Baroque grottoes.

By the end of Louis XV's reign (1715-74) the population of the city had soared to more than half a million. Thomas Girtin's exquisite view of the quai de la Grève, with its half-timbered houses, serves as a reminder that Paris was still a medieval city crammed with narrow teetering houses struggling for light above the filthy cart-tracks that served as streets below. The black market thrived and smuggling became uncontrollable, prompting the construction of another wall around another belt of land, punctuated by a series of imposing toll-houses.

In spite of the appalling conditions within the city, another architectural movement was taking hold. Under Louis XVI (1774-92) the thinking classes called for a return to a more sober classical taste. The socially responsible architects of the Enlightenment were inspired by more classically correct antique forms and motifs – the swags, trophies and medallions which they had studied at the architectural academy in Rome.

Swept up by the spirit of Romantic Neo-classicism Hubert Robert and Pierre-Antoine Demachy began to paint Paris as though it were indeed Rome, seeking subjects which allowed them to paint the city in ruins and dramatically increasing their scale. We have inherited their views of the monstrous Bastille being pulled down, the demolition of houses on the Pont au Change and the Pont Notre-Dame, and the burning of the theatre of the Opéra at the Palais-Royal.

The Revolution and the Terror stampeded through the city between 1789 and 1794, leaving no trace of the fanciful ephemeral structures which had been built in joyous celebration. Churches were demolished or deconsecrated as the Christian tradition was discarded and they were then later reconsecrated by Napoleon. The defeated emperor eventually left Paris for Elba in 1814, having bequeathed to the city his overblown Empire Style with its gigantic Roman Imperial motifs – palmettes, winged lions, laurel wreaths, fasces and bees. There were more triumphal arches, this time on the place de l'Etoile and the place du Carrousel, as well as the church of La Madeleine, a great temple in the new faubourg St-Honoré, and some splendid streets by Percier and Fontaine.

Strict rules prevented the construction of houses outside the city walls but the city's growth continued and conditions deteriorated further. Travel became almost impossible. The Bourbons were restored after the Battle of Waterloo and the so-called July Monarchy in 1830, but still no attempts were made to modernize the fabric of the city. While Haussmann was plodding away as a provincial civil servant in the Yonne district, Louis Napoleon Bonaparte was dreaming of an imperial city. From his prison cell in England, he wrote in 1842, 'I want to be a second Augustus ...Augustus...made Rome a city of marble.'

He did not build a city of marble, but he did transform Paris on an imperial scale between 1852 and 1870. Addressing the problem of lack of space and the impossibility of access, the Bonaparte-Haussmann team annexed a ring of surrounding villages including Montmartre, Belleville, Bercy and Auteuil and carved the new Paris into 20 *arrondissements*. Wide new boulevards and avenues furrowed through the ancient city, linking it to the new. But also, like mushrooms overnight, public markets, law courts, police stations, theatres, banks, churches, department stores, parks, graveyards, sewers and aqueducts, sprang up all over the city. The Louvre was finally finished after 700 years of building, and so was the Tuileries Palace, only to be burnt out during the Commune in 1871.

Second Empire architects built this new Paris in a hotchpotch of revival styles. Its most fantastic monument is Charles Garnier's Opera House. When Empress Eugénie saw the designs she exclaimed, 'It is neither Greek, Roman, nor Louis XIV, nor Louis XV!', to which Garnier replied, 'It is Napoleon III, Your Majesty.' Nineteenth-century French architecture was further complicated by the onset of the Gothic Revival, which was spearheaded by Eugène-Emanuel Viollet-le-Duc. This famous revivalist made swingeing alterations to Notre-Dame in the name of restoration and called on

French architects to return to their native architectural style and throw off the yoke of Italian influence.

Haussmann's works transformed Paris socially too. 25,000 people were evicted from the Ile de la Cité alone, and its streets were reduced from nearly 100 to just 16. Thousands of tenants found their buildings condemned. If poor, they migrated to the city limits where new factories were being built. If they had got rich quick through compensation or speculation, they moved to the new *beaux quartiers* to the west of the city. In the mid-1860s almost 20 per cent of the workforce was employed in the building trades.

Parallel with the revolution taking place in the city's physical form, was a revolution in how it was perceived. In 1837 Daguerre invented the daguerreotype. His first subjects were sunlit buildings which could not move and reflected plenty of light. The invention caused a sensation. Ruskin said it was 'as if a magician had reduced the reality to be carried away into an enchanted land'. In 1845 Friedrich von Martens built a daguerreotype camera with the first wide-angle lens, and in 1859 Nadar flew over Paris and took the first stereoscopic aerial photograph of the city. By the 1860s cameras were focused on buildings, especially rooftops, all over the city.

Napoleon III's modern metropolis provided fascinating material for artists, draughtsmen and photographers, much as Mitterrand's Paris does today. Lavish new volumes illustrating the city's new glories, such as Labedollière's *Le Nouveau Paris* and Audiganne's *Paris dans sa splendeur*, were published to satisfy the appetites of a huge new middle class eager to see itself and its city represented. The flood of urban imagery was swelled by the debate over the destruction of old buildings and streets and an urge to record them before it was too late. But the demolition of ancient streets did not end with the Second Empire. The rue Ou Dieu Fut Bouilli ('The Street Where God Was Boiled'), one of the most historic streets in Paris, got lost when it was incorporated into the rue des Archives in 1880. Its name was derived from an anti-Semitic legend which told how a Jew named Jonathas stabbed the host which he had stolen from a chapel in the street. According to the legend, when the host bled Jonathas tried to boil it, but it rose out of the water. Jonathas was burnt at the stake on the place de Grève, a deed marked by a gory public holiday for several centuries.

As early as 1861 the poet Baudelaire announced 'the old Paris no longer exists, the form of a city changes more quickly, alas, than the heart of a mortal.' Nostalgia for the 'old Paris' sold thousands of views, such as Laurence's *Les Restes du Vieux Paris*, and etchings of the oldest quarters by Martial, Flameng and Meryon – who were sponsored by the city authorities themselves. In time, with the development of lithography, wood-engraving and photomechanical production, it became easier and cheaper to produce familiar sights.

Instead of giving in to photography, the Impressionists determined to create the opposite effect. Their street views deliberately eschewed minute detail in favour of forming an atmosphere, an impression. They transformed an imagery, which had been the province of topographers and illustrators since the days of Chastillon, into a source of inspiration for major artists and played a crucial role in making Paris a mecca for artists and writers.

The last 'Parisian' style was created by Hector Guimard in the 1880s at the beginning of the period known as the Belle Epoque. Art Nouveau was a reaction to the overblown classicism preached at the Ecole des Beaux-Arts and was named after Samuel Bing's shop 'La Maison de l'Art Nouveau', which opened in Paris in 1895. Its inspiration came from the sinuous plant and flower forms of France's Gothic and Celtic history, which had originally been derived from England and Japan.

Perhaps because of its inclination to decorate, Paris did not embrace Modernism easily. Few great architectural monuments were built in the run-up to the Great War, or between the wars. The Occupation left Paris on its knees and once again desperate for housing. Nanterre, Créteil and Bobigny became prefectures of the Parisian region and President de Gaulle's post-war *Grands Ensembles*, high-rise dormitory towns, created new social problems which remain unresolved. Not until the inauguration of the Pompidou Centre in 1977 did Paris acquire a truly startling new building. This was the catalyst which ushered in a new era of patronage. One of its most visible results is President Mitterrand's glass Pyramid at the Louvre. Another is La Grande Arche at La Défense, designed by Johann Otto von Spreckelsen, and selected by Mitterrand as an appropriate monument with which to terminate the east-west axis of the city. He chose a cube with a hole in it, a 'window onto the future', as a symbol for the possible future growth of the city.

For the visitor there is a medieval Paris and a modern Paris. In medieval Paris you only feel alive on the street. Buildings lean so close to each other that, in the breathless heat of high summer, you can't avoid noticing your neighbour's underwear, or which chat-show he is watching on TV. Pedestrians squeeze past each other on pavements scarcely wide enough for dogs. Traffic jams are constant. In this Paris people lounge in cafés, their legs sprawling across the pavements, eyeing up passers-by.

In the other Paris there are ranks of inscrutable apartment blocks in peaceful streets. Armies of immaculate Parisians commute crisply. Traffic whooshes down the wide avenues and boulevards. Instead of tiny cafés, there are glass-fronted brasseries, polished boxes where the manicured, in mustard-coloured jackets, are complimenting each other over lunch.

Each of us has his own Paris. As Hemingway reflected, 'the memory of every person who has lived in it differs from that of any other'. For anyone who has ever lived in Paris, no matter where else they go, the memory of their Paris goes with them. The latest in the endless procession of artists, writers and photographers, Matthew Weinreb has looked anew at Paris and in this book he offers you the city as it appeared through his lens, as an encouragement to go forth and discover a Paris of your own.

Fiona Biddulph, 1994

The Island

Little remains of the old Ile de la Cité, the ancient heart of Paris, once a mass of closely interwoven streets ensnaring Notre-Dame. In 1852 Georges Eugène Haussmann gutted this area in the name of 'hygienization'. Apart from the Sainte Chapelle and Notre-Dame, the only medieval corner of the island still intact today encompasses about half a dozen narrow little streets between the cathedral and the quai aux Fleurs, where the island's first inhabitants, the Parisii, established the city's original port.

One of these streets, the rue Chanoinesse, saw the story of Abélard and Héloïse unfold. Fulbert, Canon of Notre-Dame, lived here with the fair Héloïse (supposedly his niece), a beautiful and clever 17-year-old. In 1118 their lives were disrupted by the greatest philosopher and teacher of his age, the brilliant and irreverent Pierre Abélard, who rented rooms in their house and offered to teach Héloïse personally. Abélard, who was Héloïse's senior by 22 years, later wrote, 'Under the guise of study, we gave ourselves up to love...Love chose the mysterious retreats where the lesson hour flowed away; we exchanged more kisses than sentences...' Héloïse, needless to say, became pregnant, but she refused to marry Abélard, on the grounds that such a genius should never be burdened with responsibility. After giving birth to their child in Brittany, Héloïse returned to rue Chanoinesse where she changed her mind and married Abélard in a secret ceremony, although she decided that she would never live with him as his wife.

But Canon Fulbert began to maltreat Héloïse, until one day Abélard swept her away to a convent for protection and she became a nun. Obsessed by the desire for revenge, Fulbert sent two thugs to Abélard's house in the dead of night. They dragged him from his bed and castrated him, leaving the humiliated hero to retreat to a monastery himself and become a monk. Fulbert was punished for his actions by the loss of his canonical position and the confiscation of all his possessions. His hirelings had their eyes gouged out and were also castrated under the legal precept of talion (an eye for an eye and a tooth for a tooth). The lovers remained in separate institutions until Abélard's death, when Héloïse had his body smuggled into the nunnery. When she finally died in 1164, aged 63, she was buried in the same grave.

The delicate tracery of the Sainte Chapelle's Upper Chapel on the Ile de la Cité.

Above: Flower finials on a Gothic Revival tomb at Père-Lachaise cemetery. Père-Lachaise has been Paris's most fashionable cemetery since it was opened by Napoleon in 1804. Named after Père François de La Chaise, Louis XIV's confessor, it is richly endowed with some of the finest nineteenth- and twentieth-century funerary monuments in Europe. Abélard and Héloïse, Modigliani and Jim Morrison are among the hundreds of illustrious people who are buried here.

Right: Crisp Early Renaissance Revival decoration on a door of the Bibliothèque Ste-Geneviève, place du Panthéon. Built in 1844–50 by Henri Labrouste, the library was much acclaimed in its day for its elegant and original detailing.

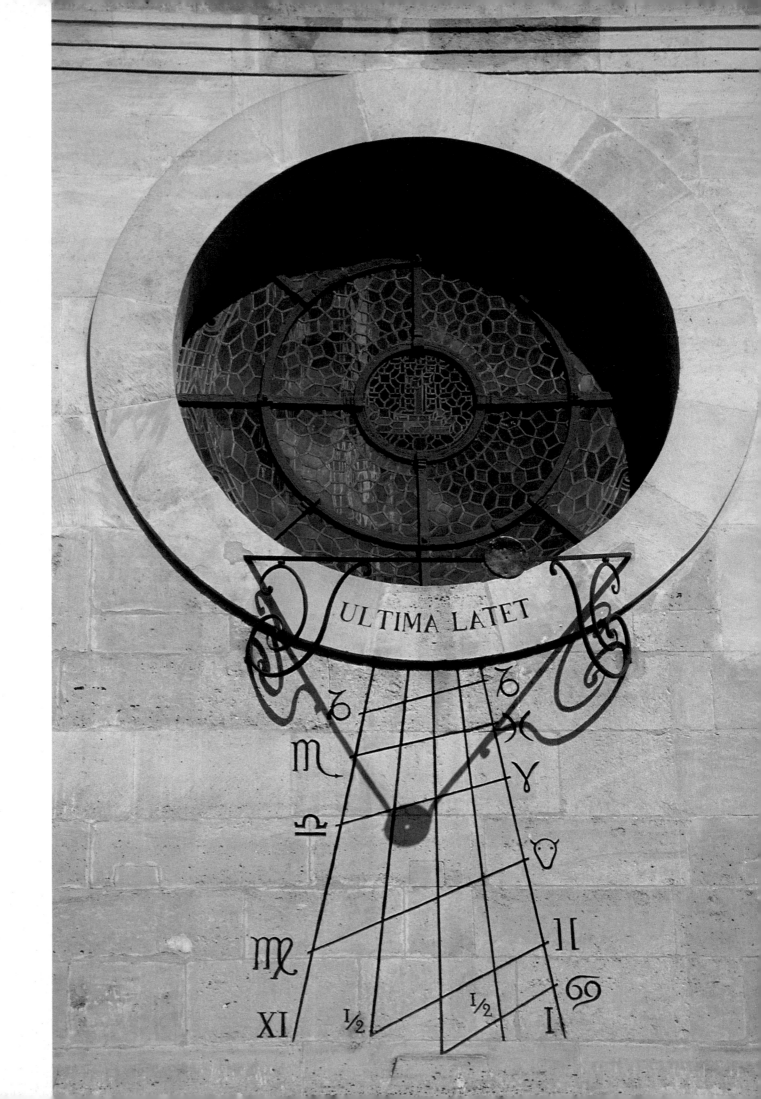

Left: The sundial at Libéral Bruant's Chapelle de St Louis de la Salpêtrière ominously warns that the end is mysterious. Built in 1660-77, the Salpêtrière was the church of the notorious Hôpital de la Pitié-Salpêtrière, an institute for elderly and insane women, foundlings and prostitutes. The hospital took its name from the saltpetre used to make explosives in a gunpowder factory formerly on the site.

Right: The interior of the Bourse du Commerce, the old corn exchange, which is now the Paris commodities exchange. Built in the mid-eighteenth century and remodelled in 1888-9, the Bourse is the only remaining relic of the Halles Centrales, the old market place, which moved out of the city to Rungis in the 1960s. Victor Hugo thought that the outside of the building looked like a jockey's cap without a peak.

Above: Balcony on the Pavillon de Flore at the Louvre. The pavilion was built during the reign of Henri IV, altered by H-M Lefuel for Napoleon III and restored between 1871 and 1076 after it had been damaged by fire.

Left: Wrought-iron balcony in place Vendôme, a superb Louis XIV square surrounded by mansions designed by J Hardouin-Mansart. Originally called the place des Conquêtes, the square took its present name from the *hôtel* built here for César, Duc de Vendôme, the illegitimate son of Henri IV and his mistress Gabrielle d'Estrées. The gilded head of Apollo in the ironwork of the balcony is a reference to Louis XIV, the Sun King, whose equestrian statue used to stand in the centre of the square.

Following pages
28 The dazzling glass facade of the Canal Plus television station headquarters, designed by Richard Meier in 1991, fronts the quai André Citroën.
20 Heavy iron balconies articulate the facade of rue de Solférino, which was laid out in 1866 as part of Baron Haussmann's grand plan for the new Paris.

The Pompidou Centre
(1972-7), designed by
Richard Rogers and Renzo
Piano. An 'inside-out'
building, the colours of the
pipes on the exterior
distinguish their different
functions. Air ducts are blue,
water pipes green and
electricity lines yellow.
The red areas are passages or
lifts. In a 1986 poll taken
from 99 French architects,
the Pompidou Centre was
voted the most important
contemporary design in
France and Piano and Rogers
were deemed to be the
second most important
architects after Le Corbusier.

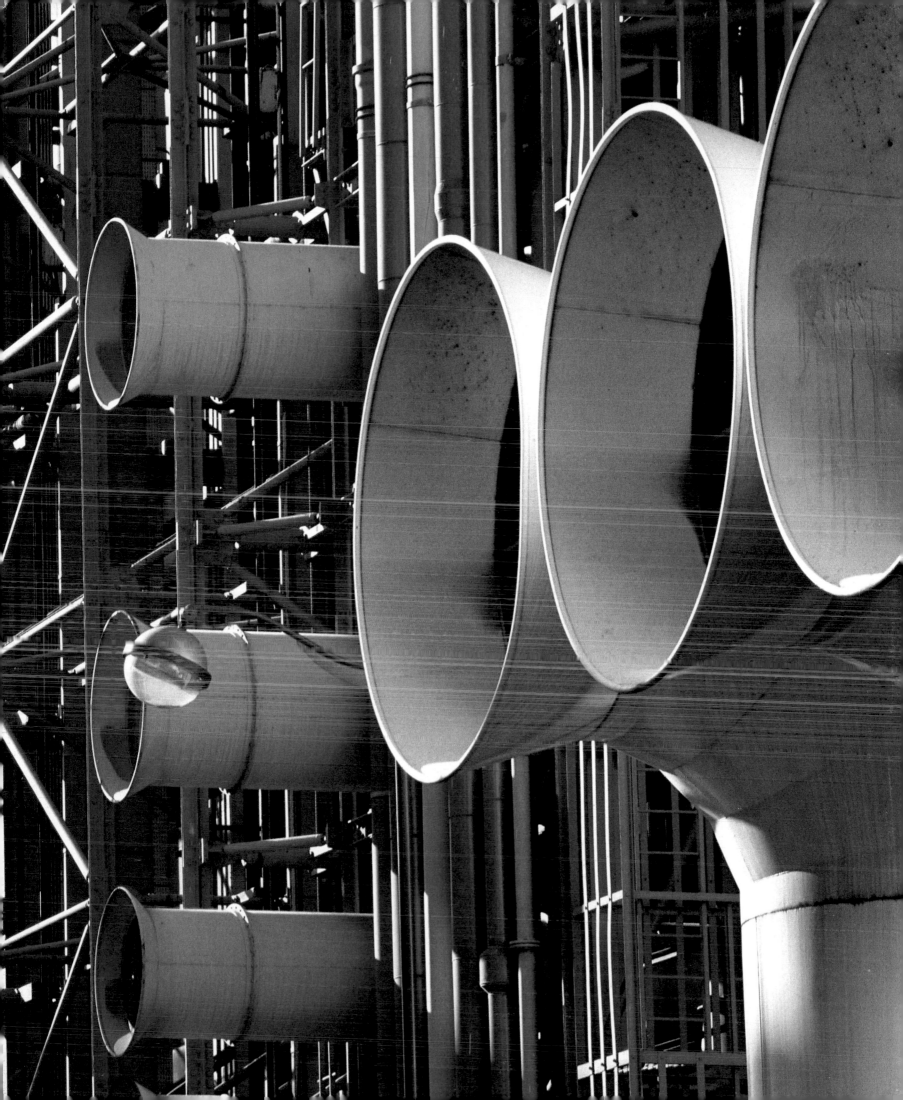

The Fortifications

'The banks of the island were her first walls and the Seine her first ditch,' wrote Victor Hugo of the early days of Paris. As the city grew and spread outwards from this natural line of defence, a series of walls were built which gradually encompassed an ever-increasing area and redefined the city's limits.

One wall in particular provoked some angry reactions. From its inception in 1784 the wall built by the Ferme Générale was seen to represent an extraordinary anachronism – a brutal check on freedom of movement in a century of free trade. Smuggling caused serious loss of revenue to the Ferme Générale, the tax-collecting body which had been reorganized by Jacques Necker in 1780. Thus, in order to gather effectively the duties payable on goods entering the city, the tax farmer Lavoisier decided to build a string of toll-houses and a new wall which would surround the capital and include within it all the new faubourgs currently outside the city walls (such as the areas around the Ecole Militaire, the chaussée d'Antin and Montmartre). At the intersection of the roads into the city customs posts known as *barrières* were to be built by the leading architect of the day, Claude-Nicolas Ledoux.

The *barrières* were unpopular from the start because of their function and their appearance. William Beckford, who visited Paris in 1784, described Ledoux as 'the very prince of pomposity', and the *barrières* as 'the entrances of a necropolis...' The handful that survive today do indeed have an impenetrable quality. In their time they would have looked like lighthouses disguised as an endless variety of Roman temples, littering the virgin wastes around the city. Ledoux called them '*Propylées*' after the Propylaea in Athens – but this allusion was certainly over the heads of most people. In 1787 the reviled wall was accused of impeding the circulation of fresh air through the city and, during the Revolution, some *barrières* were attacked by the mob.

Marmontel told the story of the orator who, railing against a *barrière*, described how he had seen 'the enormous head of a lion, open jawed, and vomiting chains...Is it possible to imagine a more fearful emblem of despotism and slavery?' At this point he roared at the crowd. Marmontel, who had noticed no such thing, went to have a look. Peering down he saw 'a shield suspended by a small chain which the sculptor had fixed to a little lion's muzzle, such as we see on the knocker of a door...' Despite its associations, the Ferme Générale's wall remained in place to mark the official limits of the city until the 1850s.

The Rotonde de la Villette on place Stalingrad by Ledoux.

Top: St Paul's Cathedral in London and Claude Perrault's circular peristyle around the domed chapel he planned for the Louvre are amongst the inspirations behind the dome of Soufflot's Panthéon (1764-89)

Above: The Dome IMAX at La Défense is advertised as containing the largest cinema screen in the world.

Left: The dome of Girault's Petit Palais, decorated with Beaux-Arts fish-scale tiles. Built to house a retrospective exhibition of French art at the Expo 1900, the palace now contains the collection of the Musée des Beaux-Arts de la Ville de Paris.

Left: Ornate Renaissance decoration from the facade of St-Etienne-du-Mont. *Right:* Detail of the decorative brickwork from a Belle Epoque former school in rue Rouelle, built by Bonnier in 1912.

The doors to these Parisian *hôtels particuliers* were made to order in the faubourg St-Antoine by some of the finest craftsmen in Europe.

St-Eustache is a medieval church with superimposed Renaissance decoration. Madame de Pompadour and Cardinal Richelieu were baptized here; Molière and Colbert laid to rest.

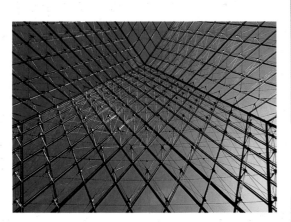

Above: I M Pei's glass Pyramid, the new focal point of the Cour Napoléon, and the entrance to the Louvre. Sensitive to the accusation that the Pyramid might distort the views of the surrounding courtyard, Pei had it constructed from specially created ultra-transparent glass.
Right: The Palais de Tokyo is in the west wing of the Palais d'Art Moderne, which was built in a stripped Classical style for the 1937 Universal Exhibition by Aubert, Dondel, Viard and Dastugue.

The Faubourgs

Faubourg is the old Parisian word for a suburb, to be distinguished from *banlieue*, which approximates more to a commuter belt. While the adjective *faubourien* is used to describe a Paris working-class accent, *Le Faubourg* or *le noble faubourg* was a reference to the faubourg St-Germain, on the left bank. This area was open country until the end of the sixteenth century but, after Henri IV built the Pont-Neuf and the rue Dauphine, it became more accessible and rich *émigrés* from the marshy land around the place Royale began to develop it as a fashionable new zone. During the reign of Louis XV, this new faubourg replaced the Marais as the aristocratic quarter. After the Revolution, some aristocratic families returned here to reclaim their former residences but to live in penury. Balzac made the point that *du Faubourg* was a definition of old school language and manners, regardless of whether the individual actually lived in the faubourg St-Germain.

In total contrast the faubourg St-Antoine on the right bank was 'the crater from which the lava of revolution erupted'. This was where Claude Santerre ran the Brasserie Hortensia, which became a conspirators' nest during the Revolution and the Terror. It was Santerre who rattled the tumbril prematurely, depriving Louis XVI of his last words to the people before he was guillotined. Justifying his action, Santerre said, 'the tyrant only wanted to trick the people yet again'.

The faubourg St-Antoine was (and still is) the territory of the woodworkers, who range from the *ébénistes* (cabinet-makers who use the finest exotic woods), to the humble *huissiers*, *châssissiers* and *huchiers* (makers of door- and window-frames, coffers and chests). The suburb grew up around the abbey of Saint-Antoine which granted the guild the right to work the church's land freely. In 1657 Colbert gave the artisans exemption from all corporate regulations, which resulted in a tremendous flowering of craftsmanship. This was the quarter whose workshops produced the classic French furniture styles known as Louis XIV and Louis XV.

Unrest began to brew in 1740 when rigorous new restrictions curtailed the special privileges enjoyed by the artisans. The rabbit-warren of courtyards, passages and impasses made it easy for the rebels to erect barricades and defend themselves. In 1830 there were 29 barricades in the rue du Faubourg-St-Antoine alone. In June 1848 the entrance to the street from the place de la Bastille was blocked by a vast mountain of debris. The Archbishop of Paris, Monseigneur Affré, in a valiant attempt to stop the bloodshed, climbed onto this barricade to persuade the revolutionaries to submit, but a bullet struck him a mortal blow and he died the following day.

The doorway at 31, rue du Faubourg-St-Honoré.

Left column: Doorknockers at the Musée de la Monnaie; the Palais de Justice, and 51, rue d'Anjou.

Right column: Door furniture at 2, rue St Louis-en-l'Ile; the Petit Palais, and the Palais de Justice.

Opposite: A giant lion lolls over the doorway at the seventeenth-century Hôtel de Fieubet, square Henri Galli.

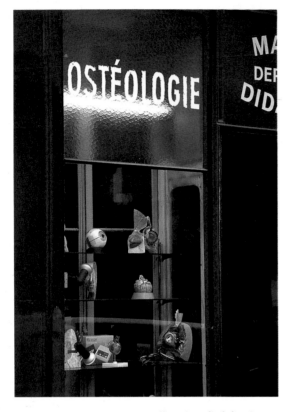

Above: A medical shop in rue Hautefeuille.
Right: A hat shop in rue Yvonne-le-Tac. Blue enamel street signs were put up all over the city in 1844. Until then street names had been carved into the stone.

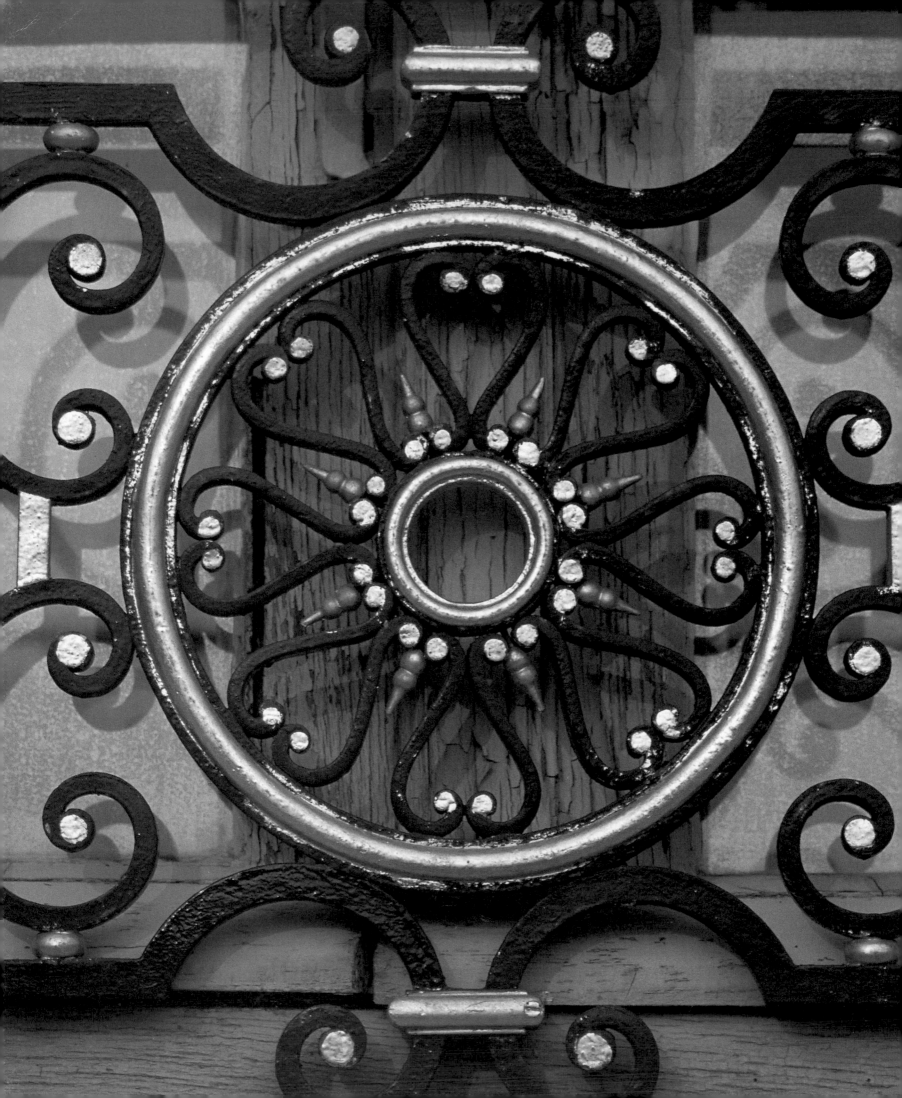

Top left: Oeil-de-boeuf window festooned with ribboned laurels above a door in rue des Archives. The keystone bears a mask of Mercury, herald to the gods.
Below left: Louis XIII oeil-de-boeuf window above a door at the Musée Adam Mickiewicz on the quai d'Orléans. Here the laurels, which are much more compact, form a pulvinated frieze.
Opposite: Detail from a balcony at the Hôtel Biron (Musée Rodin), which was built in 1728-30 by Aubert after designs by Jacques Gabriel. Rodin was living here when the state bought the house in 1901. In exchange for the right to remain, he agreed to leave the state his entire oeuvre on condition that it remained in this house.

Following pages
52/53 Pierre Mignard's magnificent *Apotheosis of St Anne* in the cupola of the Val-de-Grâce contains over 200 triple-life-size figures. The church was commissioned by Anne of Austria in thanksgiving for the birth of her son after 22 childless years of marriage.
54/55 Johann Otto von Spreckelsen's Grande Arche at La Défense, as seen from below. It is made from Carrara marble, grey granite and reflective glass. The screen suspended beneath it is called the *'nuage'* and was added by Peter Rice in 1987 after von Spreckelsen's death.

The Great Exhibitions

Napoleon III gazed across the Channel at the Great Universal Exhibition of 1851 and decided that this would be the perfect way to consolidate his own position in Europe. Thus began a series of international trade fairs which was dedicated to the concept of Progress – its heroes were the inventors. From 1855 to 1937, the world came to Paris to make discoveries: aluminium, photography, sewing-machines, lifts, refrigerators, electricity and centrifugal forces. In his *Dictionnaire des Idées Reçues*, Gustave Flaubert defined *exposition* as the '*sujet de délire du XIXième siècle*'.

The first expo was held in 1855 on the carré de Marigny and the cours la Reine. The second took place in 1867 on the Champ-de-Mars, a military parade ground situated on the left bank between the Seine and the Ecole Militaire, which had been converted into a racecourse under the Restoration. The site was impregnated with significance. The Revolutionary Fête de la Fédération was held there in 1790, and Robespierre's Fête de l'Etre Suprême in 1794.

As the Great Exhibitions became ever more extravagant, they devoured more and more of the land surrounding their sites. In 1878 the Butte Chaillot, on the other side of the Seine from the Champ-de-Mars, was colonized. In 1889 the zone from the Champ-de-Mars to the Esplanade of the Invalides was drawn into the exhibition complex and, in 1900, so too was the strip along the right bank of the Seine which had hosted the 1855 exhibition. The last expo, held in 1937, linked the sites of the Grand and Petit Palais with the old Butte Chaillot, together with the quai de New York.

Napoleon III was determined to make the expos architectural showcases. As soon as he had set eyes on Joseph Paxton's Crystal Palace, he wanted one of his own and commissioned two French architects, Viel and Desjardin, to construct their version. Thereafter each successive expo produced acre upon acre of fantastic modern buildings, intended to show off the technological wizardry of every nation. More often than not, however, all they succeeded in creating was a vulgar display of buildings clad in national fancy dress.

The constructions were meant to be temporary. Those that remain – the Palais du Trocadéro (built in 1878 and replaced by the Palais de Chaillot in 1937), the Eiffel Tower (1889), the Grand Palais, Petit Palais and Pont Alexandre-III (1900) – were all by French architects. The building with the most international significance was the tower built by Gustave Eiffel, the grandfather of French high tech.

The enormous glass and iron dome of the Grand Palais.

Left: Behind the Classical facade of St-Gervais-St-Protais, with its three tiers of paired Doric, Ionic and Corinthian columns, lies a soaring Gothic interior.

Right: The fretted spiral staircase of St-Etienne-du-Mont, possibly by Philibert de l'Orme, is a masterpiece of French Renaissance stone-carving. The church has both Gothic and Renaissance elements; its construction spanned almost 100 years, from 1492 to 1586.

Following pages

60/61 The mighty vault of the Arc de Triomphe with its tough, hard-edged coffering is symbolic of Napoleon's imperial aspirations. Its sheer scale recalls the spirit of the Italian architect and archaeologist, Giovanni Battista Piranesi.

82/63 The keystone of an arch provides the perfect opportunity to create an arresting and decorative focal point.

Above: Detail from the facade of the Art Nouveau church St-Jean l'Evangéliste (1894-1904), designed in the Islamic style by Anatole de Baudot.

Left: Mosaic and brick create richly textured geometric patterns on the walls of Bonnier's former Roman Catholic school in rue Rouelle. The chevron pattern is reminiscent of French Romanesque architecture, which was fashionable from the mid nineteenth century onwards.

Following pages
66/67 The crossing of the church of St-Paul-St-Louis, the earliest example of Jesuit architecture in France. The church was built for Louis XIII between 1627-41 by Père François Derrand, a Jesuit architect.

Gateways and Doors

One of the greatest joys which Paris offers the stroller is a cornucopia of richly carved *portes-cochères* or gateways. From the earliest days of the *hôtel particulier*, architects used the *portes-cochères* (which were wide enough to let a carriage through), as a screen onto which to project their skill at ornamentation. Decoration on domestic architecture was designed according to a strictly regulated code, the rules of *Convenance* or the suitability of certain types of decoration to social status. Thus the decoration on the entrance to a nobleman's house was deemed unsuitable for a master-craftsman. Architectural treatises, such as Pierre Le Muet's *Manière de bien bastir pour toutes sortes de personnes* (published in 1623 and 1647), were quite specific about *Convenance*.

The most fantastic *portes-cochères* were constructed during the seventeenth century when French architects were perfecting the decorative vocabulary of the Italian High Renaissance and treating it in a new and French way. Masks of bacchantes, gods and the ubiquitous lion were used for keystones, medallions and panels and framed with rich borders of beribboned oak and laurel garlands. Voltaire pronounced that the art of sculpture had reached perfection under Louis XIV, the age of the snarling lion, the symbol of strength and courage, which had then been replaced by the undulating lines of the elaborately moulded shell.

The Marais is the best place to find fine seventeenth-century doorways, executed in stone, wood and stucco. One stunning example is the *porte-cochère* at the Hôtel Amelot de Bisseuil, in the rue Vieille-du-Temple. Better known as the Hôtel des Ambassadeurs de Hollande, it passed into the hands of Jacques Amelot, Vicomte de Bisseuil, in 1655. Between 1657 and 1660 the architect Pierre Cottard reconstructed the main part of the old *hôtel* for him and employed Thomas Regnaudin as the sculptor.

The sculptural decoration of the *porte-cochère* is the most striking feature of that part of the street. Heavy double doors are surmounted by a great arched tympanum containing stone figures of Fame on either side of a medallion. The doors are divided into decoratively framed panels filled with bas-reliefs. Two circular medallions depict women accompanied by the symbols of Wisdom and Abundance. Two rectangular bas-reliefs show putti holding cartouches with lions on either side. At waist-height the eye finally comes to rest on two fierce Medusa masks in oval medallions, designed to frighten off anyone who should dare to harm the inhabitants.

This lion mask is a copy of a Neo-classical doorknocker from the Hôtel des Monnaies.

A Neo-classical Fame on a spandrel at the Légion d'Honneur, the former Hôtel de Salm, which was built by Pierre Rousseau in 1784 for Prince Frederick III of Salm-Kyrbourg. The Légion d'Honneur bought the building in 1804.

Following pages
72/73 The brilliantly coloured glass skylight of Paul Sedille's Printemps on the boulevard Haussmann. Built between 1881 and 1889, it is one of Paris's most famous late nineteenth-century department stores.

Opposite top right: The original spire of Notre-Dame was destroyed in the eighteenth century. This one was built by Eugène Viollet-le-Duc in 1860.

Opposite bottom right: The rocket-like spire of Ste-Odile, which was built between 1938 and 1946.

Opposite top left: A cartouche on the pediment of the Mairie of the 14th arr bears the arms of Paris – a vessel on the sea.

Opposite bottom left: The tower atop the Mairie of the 12th arr.

Right: The tower of the steam laundry in the avenue Jean-Jaurès.

Following pages

76 A lion mask at the centre of a muscular Second Empire door grille in rue de Montmorency.

77 A winged head amidst sinuous scrollwork on a tomb in Père-Lachaise cemetery.

Top: Section of the portal at the Hôtel de Soubise. Built by Delamair in 1706-12, the building is now home to the Archives Nationales. Inside, decorative cycles by Natoire, Boucher and Van Loo among others, have survived.

Above: The Cour d'Honneur facade of the Valois wing at the Palais-Royal. Begun under Louis XIII, this is the earliest part of the palace. Two of Daniel Buren's controversial columns, commissioned by Jack Lang in 1982, can be seen in the foreground.

Right: An aedicule with segmental pediment from the portico of the Val-de-Grâce (1645-67), designed by Mansart and Lemercier.

The Architecture of the Enlightenment

Although Voltaire was the only *philosophe* who showed a profound interest in architecture, it was architecture rather than sculpture or painting which mirrored the new ideas which ultimately culminated in the outbreak of Revolution. This was in part due to the rebellion of the intelligentsia against what they saw as the trivialization of architecture to the status of mere decoration under the degenerate influence of the Rococo architects Oppenord and Meissonnier. Encouraged by Abel Poisson, the Superintendent of the King's works (who had been installed in this plum job by his sister, Madame de Pompadour), 'people of taste' called for a return to the standards of the reign of Louis XIV.

The building which best expresses the spirit of the age is Jacques-Germain Soufflot's Ste-Geneviève. Soufflot was commissioned to execute the building, in thanksgiving for Louis XVI's recovery from an illness, by the Marquis de Marigny, whom he had accompanied to Rome on a crash-course in classical architecture. Although the project was intended to strengthen the faith of the people at a time when their patience with all established authority was running out, it actually succeeded in becoming a metaphor for the rejection of the Church. Instead of following the traditional Jesuit design of St-Roch, which was based on the Gesù in Rome and had a long nave punctuated by side chapels and scrolled flying buttresses left visible on the facade, Soufflot created a centralized building with a 24-columned portico. Pilasters were banished and replaced by row upon row of colonnades. The great dome was surmounted by a statue of St Geneviève, the patron saint of Paris and the church was dubbed the '*temple de Ste-Geneviève*'.

A few years later the Jesuit Order was expelled from France and in 1791 Ste-Geneviève was secularized. Renamed the Panthéon, it now became a vast sarcophagus housing France's new saints – Rousseau, Voltaire, Gambetta, Zola and Jaurès.

The Panthéon still holds political significance. On the morning of his investiture, President Mitterrand made an unaccompanied (except by crews from all the national television stations) pilgrimage up the steps of the Panthéon to commune with the great spirits in its inner sanctuary. When he came out, he stood on the steps in the pouring rain while the Paris orchestra played Berlioz's *Marseillaise*. *Le Monde* called the performance an 'act of faith'.

The crossing of the Panthéon, designed by Jacques-Germain Soufflot.

Left: The Baroque dome of the Val-de-Grâce is one of the most decorative in the city. Children bearing flaming urns and the fleur-de-lys, the emblem of the French kings, surmount 13 windows. The monogram, an intertwined AL, is almost certainly an allusion to Anne of Austria and Louis XIV. At 40 metres high, this dome is the third highest in Paris, after the Panthéon and the Dôme des Invalides.

Right: The Dôme des Invalides was added to the church of St Louis between 1675 and 1706. Designed by J Hardouin-Mansart and completed by Robert de Cotte, the church served as a royal chapel. The lantern which tops the dome had four statues of the Virtues in gilded lead prior to the Revolution, when they were removed and melted down.

The drum of the Sacré-
Coeur's ovoid dome was
designed by Paul Abadie,
who mastered the vocabulary
of Perigordian Romanesque
whilst restoring churches in
the region.

Following pages
86 Columns from the
portico of the Panthéon.
The portico has 24
freestanding columns,
which create the effect of a
French-style ancient temple.
The inscription on the
entablature, which reads
*'Aux Grands Hommes de la
Patrie Reconnaissante'*,
was added in 1791 when it
was decided to use the
building as the burial place
for distinguished citizens.
87 The west end of the rue
de Rivoli, opposite the
Jardin des Tuileries, was
designed by Napoleon's
favourite architects, Charles
Percier and P F L Fontaine.
The Italianate style of the
architecture shows a move
away from the Empire style
and towards the Renaissance
Revival of the second quarter
of the nineteenth century.

Left: The Pont Alexandre-III, built for the 1900 Universal Exhibition, is encrusted with heavy Louis XIV-style decoration designed by Cassien-Bernard and Cousin. *Right:* Charles Garnier's Opera House (1861-75) is a Second Empire masterpiece of decorative fantasy. These bronze Vestal Virgin lamps are by Chabaud.

Above: Ionic caryatids in rue Monge.

Left: Statues of eminent Frenchmen on the Renaissance-style facade of the Hôtel de Ville, rebuilt in 1873-92 by Ballu and Deperthes following a fire begun by the Communards. In 1357 the municipal authority of Paris bought a mansion on this site for its meetings and in 1532 Domenico da Cortona, 'le Boccador', designed the original building of which this is a copy.

The Bridges

There are 35 bridges spanning the Seine within the city of Paris (including Neuilly). The oldest is the Pont-Neuf, which was begun by Henri III on 31 May 1578, an unhappy day for the king. According to legend, he cried throughout the ceremony of the laying of the first stone, thinking not of the historic moment but of his two favourites, Quelus and Margiron, who had killed each other in a duel and been buried that very morning. The miserable crowd, who stood in the rain and watched the king weeping, are said to have pronounced *'il pleurait; il pleuvait'*, and baptized the new bridge the Pont des Pleurs.

Henri's bridge was cluttered with houses and finished with triumphal arches at either end, which served defensive as well as decorative purposes. But the bridge which crosses the river today, intersecting the triangular tip of the Ile de la Cité, looks nothing like it. Henri IV and Baptiste du Cerceau carried on with Henri III's building programme and linked the university quarters with the place Royale and the Ile de la Cité. They transformed the medieval bridge into one of a magnificently sleek and modern design, devoid of houses, with wide pavements and a series of crescent moon-shaped projecting bays which were both ornamental and practical.

The bays soon attracted a motley crew of buffoons and street pedlars selling goods which ranged from books and wax figurines to spice-cake and all kinds of refreshment. There were also tooth-pullers, who converted the bays into stalls or booths by setting up trestles across the entrances.

In 1604 Marie de Médicis paid for an equestrian statue of the king to be erected at the centre of the bridge where it cut across the island. The area around the statue teemed with every sort of swindler and brigand, collectively known as the *officiers du Pont-Neuf* or the *courtisans du cheval de bronze*.

The antiquity of the Pont-Neuf, and the fact that it still retains its original character, has given rise to a number of expressions. The most common of these is *'se porter comme le Pont-Neuf'*, a Parisian equivalent of 'to be hale and hearty'. A less familiar usage comes from the days when Henri's statue attracted 'singers of new songs', who sold songsheets to the surrounding crowds for a couple of sous. If Arthur Pougin's *Dictionnaire du Théâtre* (1889) is anything to go by, the crowds must have been pretty undiscerning. Pougin described the songs thus: '*Pont-Neuf*: word used to describe a flat, trivial and altogether colourless tune.'

The Pont Alexandre-III, a technological wonder, was created by the engineers Resal and Alby.

Top: Massive Italianate stone supports in rue du Mont-Thabor.

Above: This facade in boulevard Haussmann is enriched by densely scrolling *ferronneries*.

Right: In rue Tronchet the effect of this metal balcony is less that of a screen than of a balustrade made of stone.

Following pages

96 Graceful ceramic tiles on the exterior of the minaret at the Mosquée de Paris, an Hispano-Moresque style building of the 1920s.

97 The mighty iron gateway to a bank in the boulevard des Italiens.

98 The stately east end of the rue de Vaugirard. The longest street in Paris, it follows the route of the old Roman road from Lutèce to Dreux. It was called Vaugirard after the village to which the road led in the Middle Ages.

99 An enfilade of lamps hanging in one of the peristyles bordering the gardens of the Palais-Royal. The lanterns have discreet Neo-classical details, including anthemion leaves and pine cone finials.

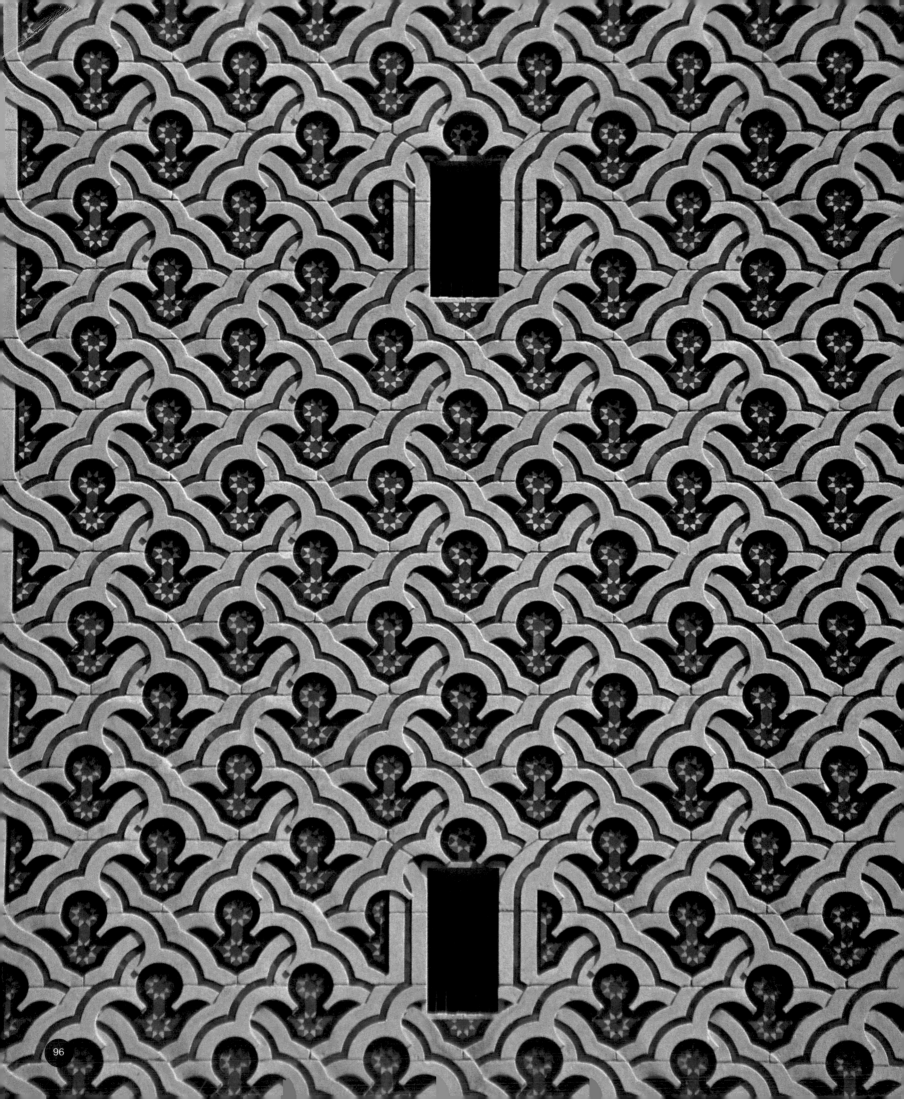

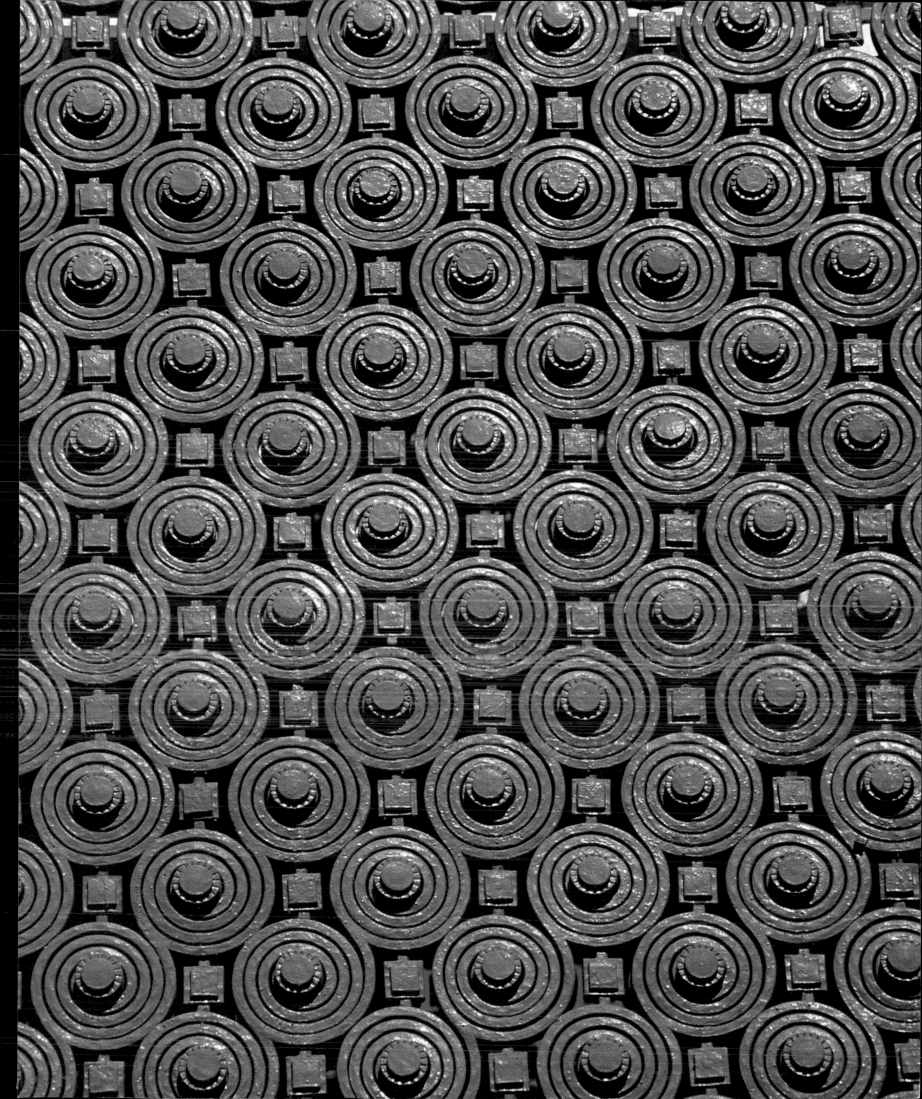

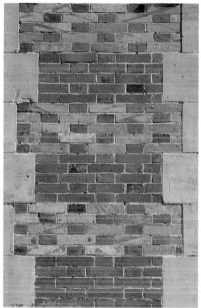

Top: Detail of the distinctive stoneware decoration on the facade of 25 bis, rue Franklin, a reinforced concrete apartment block built by Auguste Perret in 1902.
Above: Brickwork in the avenue Gordon Bennett.
Left: Mouldings on a door at La Madeleine, the church in the form of a Greek temple which was built by Napoleon to honour the Grande Armée.

Following pages
102/103 A section from one of the 15 stained-glass windows which flood the Sainte Chapelle's Upper Chapel with colour.

101

The Cemeteries

Until Napoleon I banned burials within the densely populated centre of Paris, ordinary Parisians were buried in mass charity graves in their parish cemeteries. Often no more than open ditches, these graves emitted a continual, pestilential stench.

The nastiest was the Innocents cemetery off the rue St Denis. More than two million Parisians decomposed into its earth over eight centuries. A legend grew up that the soil of the cemetery was so good it could eat up a body in nine days. Others were convinced that it could absorb them in only 24 hours. This may have been why Louis de Beaumont, buried at Notre-Dame after his death in 1492, asked to have a handful of soil from the Innocents thrown into his coffin. But in the Middle Ages this gruesome place was open ground. Children played here, laundry women hung out their washing and pigs and dogs scratched for food.

At the beginning of the fourteenth century the walls which surrounded the cemetery were extended to include an inner wall pierced with Gothic arcades. Between them a gallery was formed with ogive vaults and an attic above. This soon became the real mass grave. Scores of bones, more or less fleshless, were crammed into the attic to make room for others in the ditches below. To improve ventilation and dry the bones, the tiles were sometimes left off the roof.

The great curiosity of the arcades was a cycle of wall paintings known as the *Danse Macabre*, which was painted by a member of the Duc de Berry's circle between 1423 and 1424. The series depicted a procession of 30 dead in grimacing conversation with 30 living. The theme was how death strikes all social classes. The charnel house galleries were a notorious thoroughfare. Pedlars sold underwear and hosiery, and public letter-writers announced the price of love letters. Some even used the tombs as stalls.

In spite of the destruction of the *Danse Macabre* to make way for the extension of the rue de Saint Germain-l'Auxerrois, the cemetery continued to be used, becoming increasingly intolerable until the tenants of a house in the rue de la Lingerie nearly died from inhaling putrid emanations in December 1780. Pourtrain, the last *chef des fossoyeurs*, had buried 90,000 people during his 30 years on the job and eventually they began to ooze out. The Innocents was closed and in 1785 its remains were exhumed and taken to the Catacombs at Montrouge, a vast underground charnel-house of bones from disused cemeteries which opened in 1786.

The entrance to the Ponsat family tomb at Père-Lachaise cemetery.

A door in rue Rambuteau *(top)* and the entrance to 5, boulevard Henri IV *(above)*. *Right:* Entrance to the Ecole Nationale de la France d'outre-mer, built in the Moorish style by Adolphe Yvon in 1896.

Left: A simple lantern casts its shadow on the wall beside a beautifully proportioned door.
Opposite: Baseless Tuscan columns, justifying a heavy Doric cornice, frame a trabeated window on the first storey of Ledoux's Barrière de la Villette. This is French Neo-classicism at its starkest.

Following pages
110 Belle Epoque lettering in mosaic on rue Perrée *(above)* and *(below)* at 8, rue des Deux-Ponts on the Ile St Louis. Listed below the sign are the old charges for the public baths: *'Plein tarif 0,75: Familles nombreuses 0,40: Militaires 0,10'*.
111 Commercial lettering in rue Richer *(above)* and *(below)* rue des Gravilliers.

Above left: François I-style grille from the door of 13, rue Tronchet. It it thought that Lamennais may have lived here.

Above right: Classical grille in rue Chapon.

Left: Neat anthemions flank the numberplate at 209, boulevard St Germain.

Following pages

114/115 Marc Chagall's ceiling inside the dome of Charles Garnier's Opera House was commissioned by André Malraux in 1964. The ceiling is divided into five colours which Chagall associated with different composers: blue for Moussorgsky and Mozart; green for Wagner and Berlioz; white for Rameau and Debussy; red for Ravel and Stravinsky and yellow for Tchaikovsky and Adam.

The Fifth Republic

Georges Pompidou was the first post-war president to dedicate a monument to himself at the heart of Paris. And the Pompidou Centre, by Renzo Piano and Richard Rogers, was the first major building in Paris for two centuries not designed by a French architect. An avant-garde masterpiece beloved of both architects and the public, the Pompidou Centre set Paris on course to become the patron of some of the world's finest architects.

Valéry Giscard d'Estaing took up the architectural gauntlet, but fell from office before his projects were complete. In 1982 François Mitterrand seized his opportunity and began to litter Paris with *Grands Projets* by a galaxy of international architects. In his case there was a good reason for moving swiftly. He had only four years until the next elections; it was vital to ensure that his programme was too far advanced to be abandoned if his party were defeated.

One of the first challenges which Mitterrand faced was how to complete the world's most famous axis, which runs from place de la Concorde through the Arc de Triomphe to the area now known as La Défense. Once described by Peter Davey, the editor of the *Architectural Review*, as a 'cacophonous zoo of shambling monstrosities', La Défense is a mass of high-rise office blocks which was, in Mitterrand's view, in need of a focal point.

In 1982, with the bicentenary of 1789 looming, Mitterrand held an international architecture competition and personally chose a plan by a little-known Danish architect called Johann Otto von Spreckelsen. The result was La Grande Arche, a colossal hollow cube made out of marble and glass which now stands in pride of place at La Défense. A dazzling monument to modern architecture, the arch contains a hole so vast that Notre-Dame could be fitted within it.

Spreckelsen, who died before the arch was complete, called it 'a window onto the world...with a view to the future'. However, there has since been some debate over the choice of name and its interpretation. It invites comparison with triumphal arches and yet, unlike Paris's other arches, it is unclear what is being triumphed over here. The building is principally another office block.

The most colourful aspect of the arch is that it conceals an allegory of the Revolution. The underside of the roof is studded with the signs of the zodiac, with the lift bursting through at a particular point. Gloria Camino de Broadbent pointed out in the magazine *Architectural Design* in 1992 that, if this were a horoscope, it would belong to someone born at 2.45 pm on 14 July 1789 – 15 minutes before the storming of the Bastille.

A spectacular glass roof at La Défense.

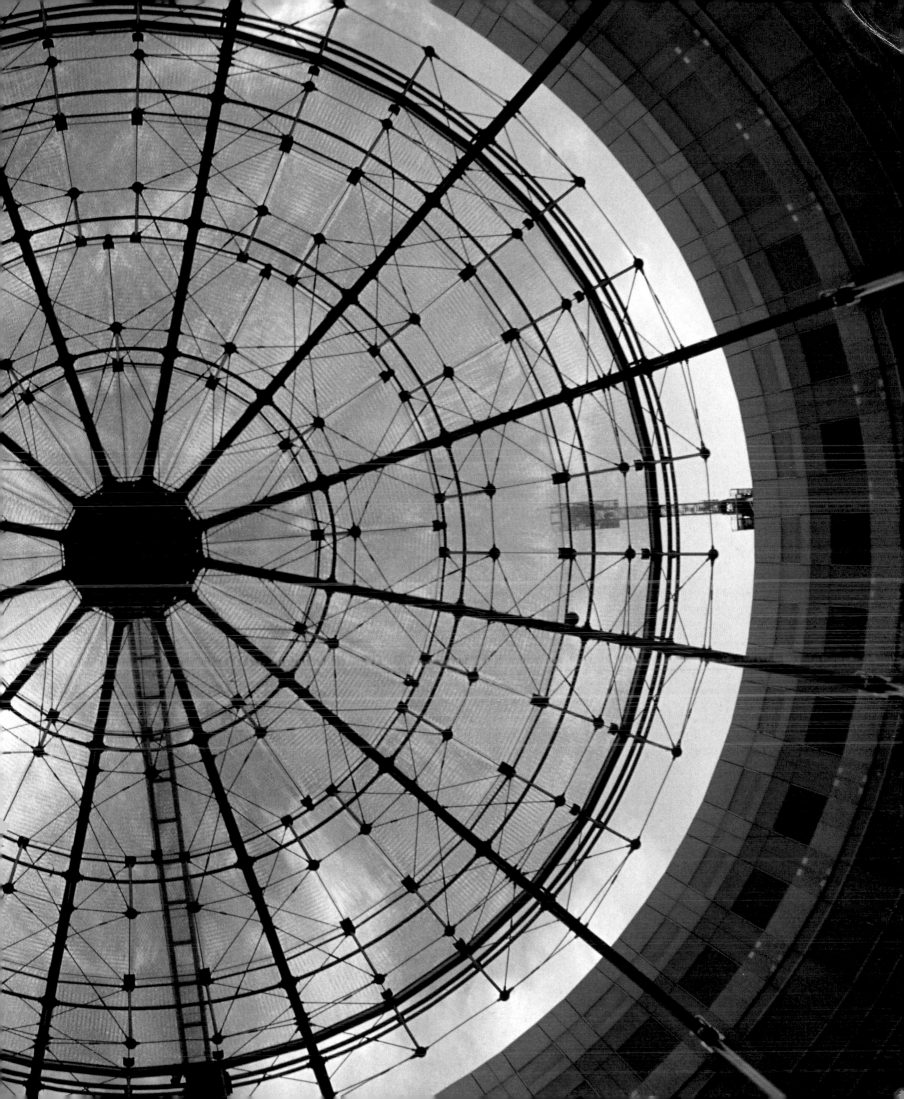

Top: A brass doorbell in rue de Seine.

Above: Carved stone lyres embellish one of the domes in the entrance colonnade of Garnier's Opera House.

Left: A plaque on the side of the Sacré-Coeur. The inscription reads *'Janua Coeli'* or 'The Gate of Heaven'.

A painted wall panel at the Sainte Chapelle. The fleur-de-lys has been the emblem of the French kings since Clovis chose it to symbolize his purification when he was baptized into the Christian church. It was also the attribute of Louis IX, who built the chapel. The castle device is the coat-of-arms of Castile or, more specifically, of Blanche of Castile, the mother of St Louis.

Following pages
122 The west front of Servandoni's St-Sulpice. The lower colonnade is Doric, the upper Ionic. Under the Convention, the church was renamed the 'Temple de la Victoire'.
123 The Ionic capitals on the facade of Girault's Grand Palais are taken from Pierre Contant d'Ivry's Cour d'Honneur at the Palais-Royal.

Left: A Greek key frieze above a decorative ironwork lunette at 156, Champs-Elysées.
Right: Brickwork from the House of the Orphan Apprentices of Auteuil, which was founded by Abbé Roussel in 1866. Abandoned children were brought here and taught skills such as carpentry, *cordonnerie* and plumbing.

Following pages
126/127 Boss framed by thick cable-moulding from the north portico to the place du Carrousel, which was added to the Louvre during the reign of Napoleon III.

Henri IV, The Builder King

From 1605 to 1610 Henri of Navarre carried out a building programme which was designed to establish Paris as the political and economic powerhouse of France. Following the Battle of Agincourt in 1415, the kings of France had ceased to use Paris as their capital. Then, between 1589 and 1594, the city had been the stronghold of Catholic rebels who refused to recognize Henri as their new king because he was a Protestant. It was only after Henri uttered his famous line 'Paris is worth a mass' and became a Catholic convert, that the city opened its gates to him. Henri's determination to make his mark on Paris can thus be understood in the light of the inauspicious circumstances which accompanied his ascension to the throne.

Projects such as the Pont-Neuf, the place and the rue Dauphine and, above all, the place Royale (renamed the place des Vosges by Napoleon) were all intended to promote commerce and link together the commercial, academic and administrative quarters of the city. The place Royale was the largest built space Parisians had ever known (and the inspiration for Inigo Jones's Covent Garden in London). Although today it is always associated with the aristocracy who took it over in the seventeenth century and made it the heart of Parisian society, Henri's original intention was that it should be a commercial centre with shops selling luxury silks beneath the arcades and accommodation for the silk-weavers above.

Acutely aware of the need to boost the country's economy after years of crippling war, Henri and his Controller General of Commerce, the Protestant Barthélemy Laffemas, planned to prevent the French from wasting currency on Italian silks by producing silk at home. Thus Henri planted mulberry trees in the gardens of the royal residences. Pamphlets were distributed explaining how city dwellers could join the effort by constructing incubators which could be used out of season as extra rooms.

Luxury workshops were established on the north side of the present place des Vosges, and Milanese weavers were installed and given every perk. In 1605 Henri announced his intention to build houses on the other three sides of the square to accommodate the craftsmen in the grandest possible style. He also planned that he himself would have a pavilion in the square to lend kudos to the new industry. The lots were leased to nobles who were to build the houses to the king's design. But the nobles did not like building such fine houses for artisans, and the artisans themselves were not happy. As a result, Henri's plan backfired and the workshops were pulled down and replaced by another row of houses.

The Pavillon de la Reine (1610) lies on the north side of the place des Vosges.

129

Above: Detail from a warehouse in Colombes, just outside Paris.
Left: Sixteenth-century door in rue Beautreillis.

Following pages
132 Shutter detail at 1, rue Bergère. The writer Gabriel Sénac de Meilhan lived here.
133 Tilework from a housing estate on the boulevard de l'Hôpital.

Right: Art Nouveau balcony in rue de Bretagne.
Opposite top: A graceful balcony in rue Monge.
Opposite below: Balcony above the door of 11 bis, rue Boissy-d'Anglas.

Following pages
136/137 Charles de la Fosse's *Glory of Paradise* billows in the cupola of the Dôme des Invalides (1675-1706). Painted in 1692, this triumphant Baroque masterpiece looks down on Napoleon's sarcophagus in the crypt below.

The south facade of Jean Nouvel's aluminium and glass Institut du Monde Arabe, the Arab public relations centre founded in 1980. The facade, which was designed to resemble Islamic lattice-work screens, is punctuated by thousands of tiny light-sensitive apertures controlled by photo-electricity. They illuminate the library by dilating and contracting according to the sun's brightness.

The Squares

Paris has always been a densely populated city, making its squares and open spaces particularly necessary. The first great *place*, Henri IV's place Royale (later known as the place des Vosges), was conceived partly in response to the people's need for some recreational ground. Louis XIV's squares, on the other hand, were designed purely as settings for his own statue: two examples are the place des Victoires and the place des Conquêtes (place Vendôme). Since the Middle Ages, the square has also served as a theatre for public spectacles. The most macabre spectacle of all was, of course, the guillotine, which was erected not only on the place Louis XV (de la Révolution and de la Concorde), but also on the place de Grève (de l'Hôtel de Ville), the place du Trône (de la Nation) and the place de la Bastille.

The present place de la Bastille was built in 1803, not on the site of the old fortress, but to the east of it, at the end of the rue St Antoine. The July Column, which has been the centrepiece of the square since 1841, has nothing to do with the Bastille. It was erected by Louis-Philippe to commemorate the 504 victims of the 1830 revolution. The victims themselves are buried beneath the column, together with the dead from the 1848 revolution.

In 1793 the 'Fountain of Regeneration', a colossal plaster statue of a seated Isis spurting water from her nipples, was erected in the centre of the square, near the ruins of the fortress. This remained in position until 1808 when the Minister of the Interior laid the foundation stone of a fountain in the form of a monumental elephant, which was designed to commemorate the fourth anniversary of Napoleon's Empire. Napoleon took a personal interest in the elephant's progress and wrote from Madrid to the minister saying 'I suppose the elephant will be very beautiful and of such vast dimensions that it will be possible to climb inside the tower that he will carry...'

In 1810 it was decided that the elephant should be encased in bronze melted down from canons seized from the Spanish and that water should spout from its trunk. A full-size model of plaster and wood (24 metres high and 16 metres long) was put up on the south side of the square and the plan was that a staircase leading to an observation platform should ascend from one of its feet. The disastrous outcome of the Peninsular War led to the project being abandoned. However, the model survived until the middle of the century, ending its days as a monstrous and unsightly rats' nest.

The elegant Doric portico of Servandoni's St-Sulpice.

Top: Detail of the basement of the colonnade on the north side of the place de la Concorde, originally the place Louis XV, which was built by Ange-Jacques Gabriel and inaugurated in 1763.
Above: Detail of the facade of the Musée d'Orsay, formerly the Gare d'Orsay. Built by Victor Laloux in 1898-1900, this was the Paris terminus of the Orléans Railway Company.
Right: Named after Napoleon's victory over the Austrians on 5 August 1796, the rue de Castiglione dates from 1802. George Orwell worked as a *'plongeur'* at No 7, the Hôtel Lotti.

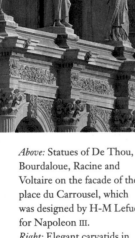

Above: Statues of De Thou, Bourdaloue, Racine and Voltaire on the facade of the place du Carrousel, which was designed by H-M Lefuel for Napoleon III.
Right: Elegant caryatids in the Jardin des Tuileries.

Following pages
146 Mask on the door of the Hôtel Lambert at 1, quai d'Anjou on the Ile St Louis. The most beautiful *hôtel particulier* built during the final months of Louis XIII's reign, the Hôtel Lambert was designed by Le Vau and decorated by Lebrun and Le Sueur for the speculator Jean-Baptiste Lambert.
147 One of the pair of Louis XIV Medusa heads carved on the doors of the Hôtel des Ambassadeurs de Hollande, rue Vieille-du-Temple. Built by Pierre Cottard in 1657-60, this was the home of Beaumarchais for 12 years and it is here that he wrote *The Marriage of Figaro*.

Above: The glass facade of the
Fiat building at La Défense.
Left: The war memorial at
St-Jean l'Evangéliste, a brick
and mosaic Art Nouveau
church designed by
Anatole de Baudot.

Above: Palmette frieze from rue Louvois.
Right: Anthemion frieze with axe heads in rue Massillon on the Ile de la Cité.

Les Grands Boulevards

At the mere mention of the word 'boulevards', many people automatically mutter the magic name Haussmann. But Baron Haussmann did not invent them. The boulevards des Italiens, St Denis, Poissonnière, St Antoine, des Capucines and de la Madeleine had all been there for nearly 200 years before Haussmann and Napoleon III replanned the city. These are the *Grands Boulevards*, which stretch along the right bank from the Bastille to the Madeleine. They are so-called because of their age and history, not their size. The word boulevard is derived from the ancient German *bohlwerk*, meaning the terreplein of a rampart. In time it came to mean a promenade encircling the city in lieu of a fortified wall: hence the *boulevard périphérique*.

The *Grands Boulevards* trace the basic lines of the fortifications set up by Charles V, the Valois and Louis XIII. After 1670 the Sun King decided that, since he had conquered all his foes, it was no longer necessary to defend the city and so he replaced the city walls with great avenues of shady trees.

The boulevards spawned a café society and a whole range of new professions, ranging from the *savoyards* who scooped out the puddles so that pedestrians did not get their feet wet crossing the street, to the mud-scrapers and waxers who cleaned and shone boots. Even those who had nothing better to do than to hang around the boulevards were given their own titles. During the Directoire, people who had got rich quick by speculation were dubbed *les incroyables*. During the Second Empire, the *lions* were the dandies of the boulevard des Italiens, while the *grisettes* were the apprentice couturiers, named after their light dress materials.

Under the Second Empire, when Haussmann was bulldozing the boulevards de Magenta, Sébastopol, Haussmann and Malesherbes through the city, Parisians began to turn west to the gardens and café-concerts in the Champs-Elysées and the Bois de Boulogne. Suddenly these were the new fashionable places to see and be seen.

The Belle Epoque was the grand finale for the *Grands Boulevards*. They had become the lively and busy quarter of popular theatre: the Comédie Française, the Opéra Comique (where Offenbach played in the orchestra whilst a student of Cherubini's at the Conservatoire), the Gaîté, the Variétés, the Vaudeville, the Renaissance (where Sarah Bernhardt took Paris by storm with her performance in *La Dame aux Camélias* in 1896) and the Funambules on the boulevard du Temple.

Skylight at the Nouvelles Galeries on the boulevard Haussmann.

Spiralling staircase at 29,
boulevard Courcelles.

Above: Detail of the dome and
roof of Printemps, Paul Sedille's
Art Nouveau department store
on boulevard Haussmann.
Left: Decorative steelwork on
the renovated interior of
La Samaritaine department
store in rue de la Monnaie.
This outstanding example of the
Art Nouveau style was built by
Frantz Jourdain in 1905.

Following pages:
158 Detail of one of the
anthemions found on an arcade
in rue des Colonnes.
159 A capital from the fontaine
Louis-le-Grand by Visconti in
the place Gaillon *(top left)*;
a vast lion capital at 39, rue
Richer *(below left)*; an aegricane
(ram's head) on an eighteenth-
century capital at the entrance
to the Galerie de la Madeleine
(top right) and a seventeenth-
century capital in the Jardin des
Tuileries *(below right).*

157

Part of James Pradier's allegorical depiction of Night and Day, which decorates the Pavillon de l'Horloge on the garden side of the Palais du Luxembourg (1615-27). The palace was built by Salomon de Brosse for Marie de Médicis in the style of the Pitti Palace in Florence. James Pradier was a Swiss Huguenot professor at the Ecole des Beaux-Arts, who drew inspiration from the work of the Della Robbia brothers.

Following pages
162/163 The Institut de France (1662-74), which stands opposite the Louvre overlooking the Seine, was designed by Le Vau in accordance with the will of Cardinal Mazarin. First known as the Collège des Quatre-Nations, students from the territories acquired by the Treaties of Münster and the Pyrenees studied here. The Institut bought the building in 1806.

Le Quartier Latin

It was the writer François Rabelais who gave the name 'Latin Quarter' to the streets where Latin was spoken, an area which extends from the *quais* on the left flanks of the islands to St-Médard and the Val-de-Grâce. To this day, Paris's most prestigious academic institutions are concentrated here and ancient religious foundations and hospitals abound. One of the least visited is the magnificent church of the Val-de-Grâce, in the south-east corner of the quarter.

The story of the Val-de-Grâce begins with Anne of Austria, the unhappy wife of Louis XIII. Aged only 19, Anne decided to create a refuge from the Louvre by buying the oratory known as the Petit-Bourbon and installing there a group of Benedictine nuns from the Abbey of Val-Profond in the Seine-et-Oise. The queen went to the convent twice a week, ostensibly to see the nuns, but really to visit secret rooms where she poured out her heart in clandestine letters to her family in Spain, the court in London and the House of Lorraine.

However, nothing escaped the eagle eye of Cardinal Richelieu and in 1637 he charged his councillor Pierre Seguier to search the premises, as well as the queen herself, if necessary. Fortunately for Anne news of the search leaked out and Seguier found nothing incriminating. Yet the king was still suspicious and forbade his wife to return to the convent.

The following year Anne gave birth to a miraculous baby, the future Louis XIV. Within five years Richelieu and her husband were dead. Free at last, she gave thanks to God by commissioning a magnificent domed church, the Val-de-Grâce. Started by François Mansart and completed by Jacques Lemercier, the building was inspired by Palladio's Il Redentore in Venice.

In 1663 Pierre Mignard painted the inside of the cupola with the celebrated *Le Séjour des Bienheureux*. Anne of Austria, led by St Louis and supported by St Anne, offers God a model of her church. Molière was so moved by this painting that he was inspired to write his only poem, entitled *La Gloire du Val-de-Grâce*.

When Anne of Austria died in 1666, her embalmed heart was laid to rest here, enveloped in lead and ruby-red cloth. During the Revolution the envelope of lead, and several others containing the hearts of Anne's descendants, were torn open and melted down at the Mint. A dozen of the hearts, including Anne's, were bought by the painter Martin Drolling to be made into mummy (a bituminous material of crushed human particles). Drolling's glaze, which was highly sought-after, was employed in a painting of a kitchen interior, which was bought by Louis XVIII and used to hang in the Louvre.

Bold lettering on a shopfront in rue Bréa.

Above: A detail of the roof of the Musée d'Orsay, which was inaugurated in December 1986. The permanent collections are mainly French works of art dating from 1848 to 1914.
Left: A gleaming façade on the quai André Citroën.

Above: Splendid lion masks and a decorative undulating band on a door of the Grand Palais.

Right: A striking balcony at Castel Berenger, the low-cost Art Nouveau apartment block which made Hector Guimard's reputation.

A section of the railway bridge connecting the 15th and 16th *arrondissements*.

171

Above right: Snarling lion mask on a doorway in the place de l'Opéra, which is contemporary with the Opera House.

Below right: Flora above the doorway to the House of Guerlain on the Champs-Elysées.

Above opposite: Macabre skull with bat's wings, imitating a winged cherub's head, on the corner of a tomb at the Père-Lachaise cemetery.

Below opposite: Carved wooden mask on a door at the Hôtel de Sully, built by Jean du Cerceau between 1624 and 1630. Sully, the minister of Henri IV, bought the *hôtel* in 1634.

173

Above: A Renaissance Revival Fame blows her trumpet in a spandrel on the Pavillon de Rohan at the Louvre. The 'N' carved on the keystone stands for Napoleon III.
Left: In 1809 Fortin added this allegory of Napoleonic victory to the central pavilion of Claude Perrault's east facade of the Louvre. Above the two winged Victories a giant inscription reads *'Liberté, Egalité, Fraternité'*.

The Butte

The Butte Montmartre is 104 metres above the level of the Seine and is the highest point in Paris. During the Roman occupation it was covered with vineyards and known as Mons Martis, Martyrum or Mercurii, either because St Denis and two of his companions had been beheaded here or because the hill had held a temple to Mercury. Apart from its redoubtable wines which were capable of inducing convulsive fits, its distinguishing feature was a collection of windmills.

Towards the end of the seventeenth century 30 windmills are mentioned, the total falling to five in 1853. The only ones to make it into the twentieth century were the Radet and the Blute-Fin. The Radet dated back to 1268, when it was built on the Butte St-Roch (since levelled by Haussmann). In 1633 the windmill was taken down and rebuilt on land belonging to the abbesses of Montmartre.

Its companion, the Blute-Fin, was owned by a dynasty of millers called Debray who passed the windmill from father to son, starting in the fourteenth century. After the Terror the Blute-Fin was converted into a *guinguette-champêtre*, an open-air music hall, where Parisian workers went to dance on Sunday afternoons. They would sit on the barrels of flour and drink milk from Pierre-Charles Debray's cows and *petit bleu* from his vines, while his wife fed them a cake known as a *galette*. Hence the windmill acquired a nickname: the Moulin-de-la-Galette.

These bucolic Sunday afternoons came to an abrupt end in March 1814, however, when the Allies attacked Paris. Under fire from Russian artillery, Joseph Bonaparte held a council of war on the first floor of the Moulin-de-la-Galette. At five o'clock in the evening, the battle was lost. A ceasefire had been declared, but Pierre-Charles, still defending his windmill, let off a volley of shots. When a Russian colonel stepped forward to protest, Pierre-Charles shot him with his pistol. Within seconds, the Frenchman was cut down by Cossacks who chopped his body into four quarters and pinned them to the ends of the mill sails. During the night, his widow took the pieces down and smuggled them, in a sack of flour, into the Calvaire graveyard by the place du Tertre.

Pierre Charles's son transformed the Moulin-de-la-Galette into a dance-hall. A few years later La Goulue, the dancer immortalized by Toulouse-Lautrec, made her debut here. The Moulin Rouge, the more famous of the two nineteenth-century windmill/dance-halls and also in Montmartre, never ground a single grain. It was an entirely bogus windmill built on the site of a demolished *guinguette* called the 'bal de la Reine-Blanche'.

The Basilique du Sacré-Coeur is the crowning glory of the Butte Montmartre.

A winged griffin, part eagle, part lion, strides down a frieze in the avenue de l'Observatoire. The motif has been taken from the Temple of Antoninus and Faustina in Rome.

179

Top: Detail of the doorway at 43, rue du Faubourg-St-Honoré. The door belongs to one of six former *hôtels particuliers* built in the street by Boullée and Boursier for the tax farmer and speculator Etienne-Michel Bouret between 1765 and 1769. Bouret ruined himself in the process.

Above: A window in the Champs-Elysées.
Right: Magnificent sculpture on the Hôtel de Fieubet by Pierre Le Muet, which was built between 1646 and 1647 for Gaspard de Fieubet, Anne of Austria's chancellor.

Above: Mosaic bucrania (ox skulls) above a door beside the main entrance to the Grand Palais. In ancient Greco-Roman ornament bucrania appeared on altars, sarcophagi and temples as sacrificial offerings and fertility symbols.

Right: Mosaic panel on the exterior of the Chambre du Commerce in rue Antoine-Bourdelle. The messenger Mercury is the traditional protector of all who are involved in trade and commerce and his symbol is the caduceus or winged staff. According to legend, Mercury threw his staff at two snakes fighting on the ground and they became entwined around it, ensuring his safe passage wherever he went.

The glass facade of La Grande Arche at La Défense.

Above: The turrets on the west end of the Hôtel de Soubise are all that remain of the Hôtel de Clisson, a medieval manor house built between 1372 and 1375 by Olivier de Clisson, one of Charles V's Constables. During the English occupation of Paris (1420-35), Thomas Duke of Clarence and the Duke of Bedford lived here.

In 1696 the site was bought by Anne de Soubise who commissioned the new *hôtel* ten years later.

Right: Detail of the roof of the Hôtel de Sens, which was built c1474-1519 as the Paris residence of the archbishops of Sens. It is now one of only two remaining examples of fifteenth-century Parisian domestic architecture. Marguerite de Valois, established here by Henri IV, used to entertain a string of young lovers in this building.

The Stations

Paris owes its railway stations to the July Monarchy (1830-48). Not wishing to be left behind in the race to lace together every town and city by mile upon mile of railway track, the great capitalists of the day encircled Paris with a constellation of six titanic termini. To make them appear less strange to a public yet to be convinced of the safety and desirability of rail travel, facades and halls were dressed up in a bracing selection of triumphal arches, pediments and pilasters.

The first four stations were the Gare de l'Est (1847-52) by F A Duquesnoy, the Gare du Nord (finished in 1847) by Léonce Reynaud, the Gare de Lyon (finished in the early 1850s) by F A Cendrier, and the Gare Montparnasse (1850-2) by Victor Lenoir. The best surviving example of an early Parisian station is the Gare de l'Est, the terminus of the Strasbourg line. By the end of the century there was also the Gare St Lazare (1885-9) by Juste Lisch, the first station to incorporate a *grand hôtel*, and the Gare d'Austerlitz by Louis Renaud.

Once early fears about train travel had been forgotten, Parisian stations began to evolve into palaces, in which great care was taken to provide comfort and luxury for the passenger. The stations symbolized adventure, escapism, the thrill of new ideas and far-off places. This feeling was reflected in their design and, above all, in their decoration. Waiting rooms became sumptuous reception areas. There were buffets and restaurants decorated by leading artists and sculptors. A new geographical iconography replaced the historical. Radiant landscapes evoked the frontiers of the empires conquered by the new princes of industry.

The supreme example of the new iconography is the turn-of-the-century Buffet at the Gare de Lyon. A profusion of elaborately gilded and twisted vegetation twines sinuously around allegories of the main stops en route to the Riviera: Lyons and Marseilles, Nîmes and Villefranche, picture-postcard renderings of the *vendages* in Burgundy and the flowers and oranges of Nice.

The age of the railway station reached its apogee in 1900, when thousands of the visitors to the Great Universal Exhibition arrived at the new Gare d'Orsay by Victor Laloux. No longer was the terminus banished to the suburb. The palace of the industrialist, constructed of iron and glass, had been given pride of place opposite the Louvre, the palace of the kings of France.

Section of the cast-iron and glass roof at the Gare de l'Est.

Top and above: These *'Filles'* and *'Garçons'* carved signs can be found at the early seventeenth-century Hôpital St Louis.

Right: Nineteenth-century grilles displaying François I-style portrait medallions in rue Ste Anne. A revival of this style was widespread in mid-nineteenth century France, when interest in what was seen as a golden period in French history was reawakened.

Above: The Hôtel Lutétia on
the boulevard Raspail is a
cocktail of Art Nouveau and
Art Deco style, designed by
Louis-Hippolyte Boileau.
It remains highly fashionable
and has recently been
redecorated by Sonia Rykiel.
Right: The Grand Rex, a
glossy club and cinema built
in 1932 by Auguste Bluysen
in collaboration with the
American picture-house
designer John Eberson.

Following pages
194 The nave of
St-Etienne-du-Mont, where
Gothic proportions fuse with
Classical forms and details.
195 The nave of the Baroque
church St-Paul-St-Louis,
which was modelled on the
Gesù church in Rome.
196 Monumental arcades
with decorative brickwork in
the avenue de l'Observatoire.
197 Arcading with giant
anthemion motifs in rue des
Colonnes.

Above: A lock from the Hôtel de Cluny, built by Jacques d'Amboise, Abbot of Cluny, at the end of the fifteenth century.
Left: Sixteenth-century choir stalls at Salomon de Brosse's church St-Gervais-St-Protais, named after two Roman soldiers who were martyred by Nero. Founded in the sixth century, it is situated in one of the earliest inhabited areas of the *Rive Droite*.

La Vie Elégante

Garnier's Opera House is rather like a crinoline. Ample and majestic, it rose, a temple to pleasure, as Paris swayed to the feverish polkas and gallops of the Second Empire. In an effort to forget the fragility of its political situation, the remorseless din of Haussmann's building and the poverty and disease still rife in the city, Paris danced.

There was the stylish Bal Mabille on the avenue Montaigne and the Château des Fleurs on the Champs-Elysées. Reputations could be made overnight by a pretty girl who could dance the polka or quadrille and gallop with brio. Céleste Venard, 'la Mogador', came out of a brothel and ended up as the Comtesse de Chabrillon. Posters everywhere advertised ballrooms: the Closerie des Lilas, the Ranelagh (where Madame Récamier had gone about practically naked in transparent shifts during the Directoire) and the Boule-Noire (where Zola's Nana made her debut). This was the age of the scandalous cancan. There was even talk of an Arabian prince who lost his reason when faced with the terrifying spectacle.

But best of all was the masked ball at the temporary opera house in rue Le Peletier. For an extortionate ten francs a ticket (half price for ladies) *grandes courtisanes* in decolletée dresses, devourers of fortunes, could rub shoulders with bankers and industrialists, German barons, Russian princes and the post-revolutionary aristocracy. The masked ball was an exceptional hunting ground for adventuresses. A B Northpeat, a visiting traveller, recounted a typical story of a naïve young man who offered to accompany a lady home in her carriage. She accepted graciously on condition that he wore a blindfold. When his blindfold was removed, he found himself in a brilliantly lit apartment in the presence of three bandits armed with *poignards* and revolvers.

When Garnier's long-awaited new Opera House was finally unveiled in 1869, it was the most lavish building of the Second Empire, constructed from stone and marble selected from more than eight different countries. On one side of the arcade opening into the vestibule the public saw a statue personifying 'Dance'. It was by the sculptor Carpeaux. In spite of the public obsession with dancing, the immodesty of the statue provoked immediate outrage. On the night of 27 August 1869 a young man, whose indignation got the better of him, hurled a pot of ink at it. The pot broke and stained the dancer's hip with ink.

A row of gilded bronze masks reigns over Charles Garnier's Opera House.

Top and above: Cherubim hover over tombs in Père-Lachaise cemetery. *Left:* Detail of a door at the Hôtel des Invalides, the great military hospital founded by Louis XIV in 1671 and constructed by Libéral Bruant and J Hardouin-Mansart.

203

Top: Clock in the pediment of the Préfecture de Police on the Ile de la Cité.

Above: Clock in a pediment on the Amphitheatre at the Jardin des Plantes. The Amphitheatre, built in 1788, used to be a lecture hall in which talks on botany and zoology were held.

Right: This magnificent round-faced clock appears on the Mairie built by the commune of Petit-Montrouge. It was added after the area had been annexed and renamed the 14th *arrondissement* under Baron Haussmann.

Above: An attenuated Art Deco centaur and faun bas-relief by Marcel Gaumont from the Palais de Tokyo *Left:* Detail from *The Peace of 1815* (1833-6) by Antoine Etex, on the western side of the Arc de Triomphe. François Rude was originally commissioned to carry out all the sculptures on the principal facades, but the lesser sculptors Etex and Jean-Pierre Cortot conspired against him and persuaded Adolphe Thiers to give three of the four to them instead. Ironically Rude's *Departure of the Volunteers of 1792 ('La Marseillaise')* is the only sculpture which has stood the test of time. *The Peace of 1815* was denounced as mediocre the day it was unveiled.

Left: Arcading in the interior of the Basilica of the Sacré-Coeur.

Right: Remarkably delicate arches spring from slender columns across the ceiling of the Reading Room at Labrouste's Bibliothèque Ste-Geneviève. Designed and built between 1844 and 1850, the library demonstrates the experimental use of exposed ironwork.

Following pages
210/211 The crossing at St-Sulpice. Although chiefly known for its early Neo-classical facade by Servandoni (1736), the interior of the church is actually earlier. Building was started in 1646 by Gamard and continued in 1655 by Le Vau, followed by Gittard in 1670 and Oppenord in 1719.

Les Beaux Quartiers

The Parisian *beaux quartiers*, as opposed to the *quartiers populaires*, have moved over the centuries from the Marais to the faubourg St-Germain. After the Revolution, *beaux quartiers* became complicated by the division of the aristocracy into pre- and post-revolutionary and by the ascending bourgeoisie. The faubourg St-Germain was still the domain of the old regime, while the faubourg St-Honoré was Napoleonic territory, although it did include the liberal nobility and rich foreigners. The chaussée d'Antin, near the *Grands Boulevards* and the Bourse, was for the *parvenus*: bankers, actresses and successful artists.

In 1859 an imperial edict permitted the annexation of villages to the west of the city, including Auteuil, Passy and Neuilly. These became the 16th and 17th *arrondissements* which Haussmann filled with row upon row of spacious new apartment blocks, with neutral facades articulated only by ribbons of shutters. The bourgeoisie flocked to the new *beaux quartiers*. With the Bois de Boulogne on their doorstep, it was like living in the country, yet they were still within easy reach of the Champs-Elysées.

New *hôtels particuliers* were built in a heavy and nostalgic Classical style (often with materials from demolished eighteenth-century *hôtels*), designed by architects such as the Destailleurs and Sanson from the Ecole des Beaux-Arts. The owners of some of these palaces were bent on outshining the *Ancien Régime*.

Yet the Palais Rose, built for count Boniface de Castellane by Sanson, surpassed all of them. De Castellane, the Belle Epoque's most extravagant arbiter of taste, was descended from an old Provençal aristocratic family and from Talleyrand. He had had the foresight to marry an American railway heiress but quickly disposed of her fortune by building an adaptation of the Grand Trianon on a half-hectare plot on the avenue Foch. This magnificent building was dubbed the Palais Rose because it had pink marble Ionic pilasters. De Castellane threw magnificent parties here at which his guests were announced by silver trumpets from the top of the stairs.

In 1906 de Castellane's wife divorced him and married his cousin. Ruined, he became a journalist and antique dealer and founded an historic house association called '*La Demeure Historique*'. In his memoirs he described his idea of paradise as a 'château in a perpetual state of construction', in a town peopled by antique dealers. During the German occupation the Palais Rose was occupied by the Nazis and in 1969 it was demolished.

Place Maréchal Juin (formerly place Pereire) was constructed in 1853. It is found in the 17th *arrondissement*.

Above: The balcony and supports at 8, rue de l'Arcade.
Right: Magnificent ironwork in rue Rambuteau.

Following pages
216 The play of light through shutters enlivens the facades of Paris.
217 *Top left:* One of the richly textured brick and stone facades of the place des Vosges, with *ferronneries*.
Below left: A twentieth-century facade seems almost naked without shutters.
Top right: Shutters, like ladders, emphasize the verticality of the walls which flank the narrow rue St Louis-en-l'Ile, the main artery which slices through the Ile St Louis.
Below right: A change of rhythm is achieved by alternating ironwork with stone balustrades in rue Rambuteau.

The Architecture of Despotism

In the fourteenth century the Bastille was a bastion (*bastille* means 'little bastion') defending the ancient porte St Antoine to the east of Paris. It evolved from a two-towered defensive post with a drawbridge into a fortress with eight towers surrounded by a moat. The notorious towers were 24 metres high and 8 metres thick. The moat, filled with water from the Seine, was 8 metres deep and 24 metres wide.

During the seventeenth century the Bastille became synonymous with political oppression. Notice of arrest of anyone thought to be of possible danger to the crown was carried out by the dreaded but completely private *lettre de cachet*. The letter was signed by the king himself and said simply 'I am writing to you in order to tell you that it is my intention that you should be taken and held there [the Château de la Bastille] in safety until I command your release.' The secrecy of the system made it easy to abuse. It was possible to buy forged *lettres de cachet* in order to condemn inconvenient relations.

It is ironic that the mob should have chosen the attacking of the Bastille as one of their first actions. During the eighteenth century the fortress was little more than a detention centre for aristocrats. Its size has also been exaggerated. There was only room for about 50 prisoners at one time which is why most stayed just a few months, or went elsewhere.

The unfortunate Marquis de Sade, imprisoned here in 1784, was sent to a madhouse on 3 July 1789 – just in time to miss a hero's liberation. Those prisoners who remained included four forgers (who were locked up again the day after they had been freed), a madman (whose family had had him committed because they considered he would be better off in the Bastille than in a lunatic asylum) and the Comte de Solages (who was thought to be unsafe on the streets because of his lascivious nature).

Although perhaps not quite a luxury hotel, prisoners were allowed their own furniture and servants and could receive visitors. By dismantling the Bastille, the mob did the Treasury a prodigious service. It cost the state a fortune to maintain, which is why Necker dreamt of closing it and replacing it with a new square, place Louis XVI. Seven of the eight towers were to be demolished whilst the eighth would have been incorporated into a structurally inconceivable pyramid of souvenirs: portcullises, bars, chains, locks and bolts. Looking on, his arm gesturing magnanimously in the direction of the demolished towers, would have been a statue of Louis XVI.

The facade of Pierre Lescot's Renaissance Cour Carrée at the Louvre, with J Lemercier's Pavillon Sully in the centre.

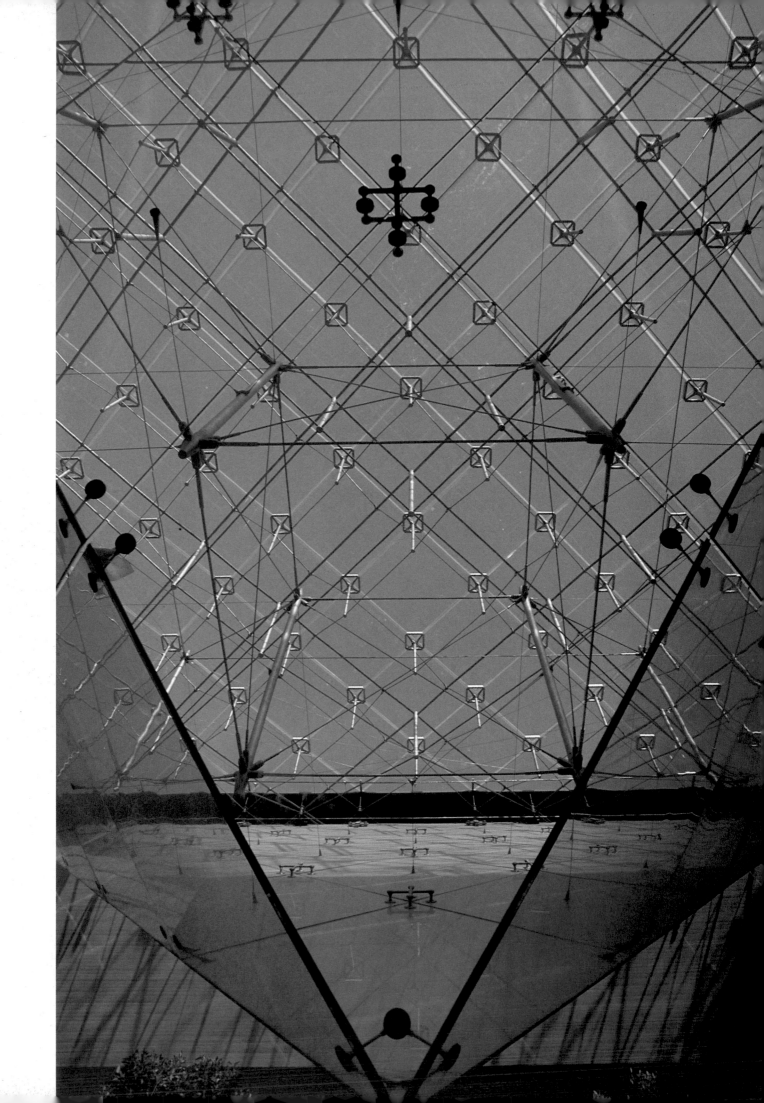

Left: I M Pei's inverse Pyramid, a suspended glass prism, lights the underground service area at the Louvre and illuminates the fragments of Charles V's fourteenth-century fortifications, which were uncovered during excavations.
Right: The roof of Jacob Hittorff's train shed at the rebuilt Gare du Nord (1863) – an early experiment in building with cast-iron and glass.

Above: The Pont de Bercy, built in 1864.
Left: Ranks of windows along a facade at the Palais-Royal.

La Voie Triomphale

When Napoleon commanded the building of triumphal arches on the place de l'Etoile and the place du Carrousel to commemorate his victories and create a triumphal route down the Champs-Elysées to the Louvre, he was not doing anything particularly innovative.

There had been a *'voie royale'* into Paris along the rue St Denis, the old road to England and Flanders, since the Roman occupation. The kings and queens of France paraded down it on their way to Notre-Dame. And, with perfect symmetry, when they died their mortal remains travelled back up the road again from Notre-Dame to the Basilica.

Triumphal entries took considerable planning. Makeshift triumphal arches straddled the path; wine and milk flowed from public fountains, while mystery plays were performed at the principal roundabouts along the route. One of the best performances was put on by Louis XI, who paraded into the city on 31 August 1461 preceded by a group of fifteenth-century cheerleaders: five young girls adorned with splendid raiments and mounted on magnificently caparisoned horses. Each one held a banner inscribed with one of the five letters which make up the word PARIS. But when Louis XVIII came through on 3 May 1814 he struck a more sombre note with his escort of soldiers from the old Imperial Guard and crowds of old soldiers lined the route and wept, shouting *'Vive le Roi!'*

The temporary triumphal arches were replaced in 1672 by two great stone arches, constructed at public expense to the greater glory of Louis XIV by the architect François Blondel. The grander arch, at the intersection of the boulevard St Denis and the rue St Denis, is known as Porte St Denis. The bas-reliefs were designed by Girardon and executed by the Anguier brothers. The one on the north face depicts the *Prise de Maastricht* and the one on the south the *Passage du Rhin à Tholus*. A pair of shallow triumphal pyramids covered with trophies flank the arch on the north side, while on the south face a personification of a consternated Holland and the vanquished Rhine appear.

Napoleon, jealous of the Porte St Denis, and wishing to turn the eyes of Parisians west towards his new arch at l'Etoile, commissioned the restoration of Louis's arch in 1807. But instead of re-gilding the words Ludovico Magno which surmount the arch and which he found far too glittery, he decided to bronze them instead. No doubt the point was quite lost on Queen Victoria, the last monarch to enter Paris by the Porte St Denis. She passed beneath it on her way to see the Great Universal Exhibition in 1855.

One of the smaller arches of the Arc de Triomphe.

Above: Gustave Michel's statue of Christ appears on the pediment of the Sacré-Coeur, completing the facade.

Right: Venetian mosaic of the tragic lovers Orpheus and Eurydice, found in the ceiling of the first-floor vestibule at the Opera House. Charles Garnier went to Italy in search of a mosaicist to execute the work because he was determined mosaic should have a role to play in French architecture, as it had done in Greek and Roman. The mosaics were eventually carried out by a Venetian mosaic floor-layer, Facchina, after drawings by Curzon.

Following pages

228/229 The Eiffel Tower, viewed from below. The complex pattern of pig-iron girders is not just a decorative device, but serves to stabilize the structure in fierce winds.

230 Kisho Kurokawa's Japan Tower at La Défense. A staircase runs through the building and leads to the bridge, which was inspired by the traditional round-backed bridges of Japan.

231 Detail of the Totem building (1978) by Pierre Parat and Michel Andrault on the quai de Grenelle. Luxury apartments cling to steel structural posts in groups of three, set at 45° angles to allow everyone panoramic views of the Seine.

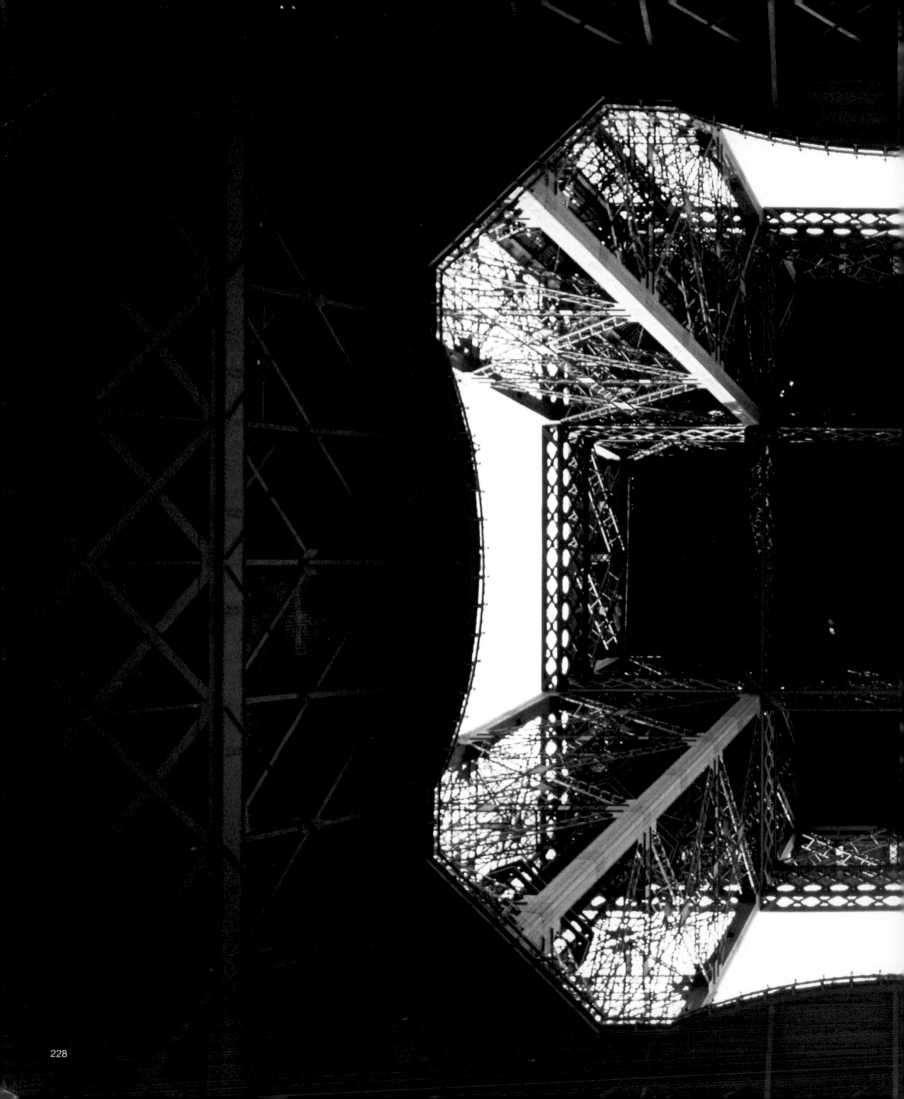

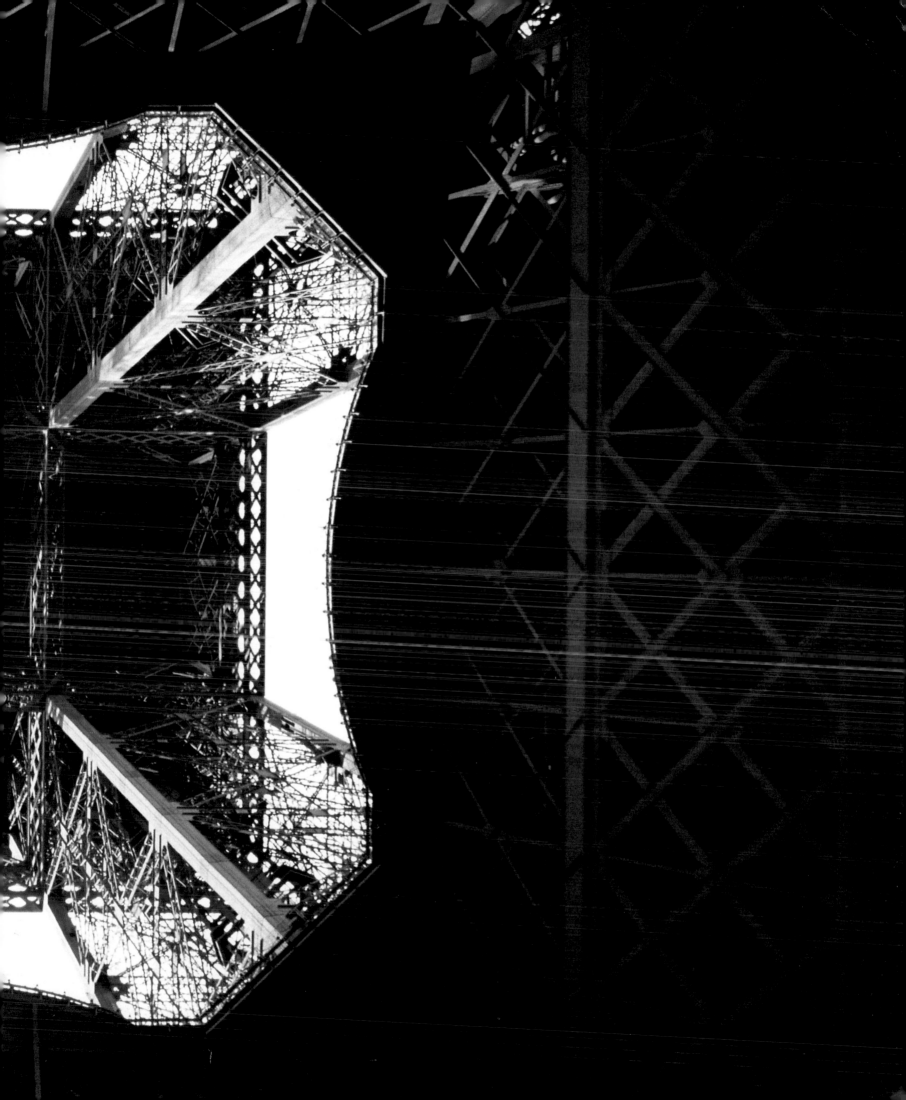

Above: Detail of heavy coffering from the vault of the Arc de Triomphe. Bound laurel leaves symbolized resurrection and glory in the Greco-Roman world. They are used here to honour the eternal memory of Napoleon and his military achievements.

Left: The angel replaces an oculus in this side-chapel dome at the Panthéon, formerly Ste-Geneviève. The most important Neo-classical building in France, the architectural quality of the decoration is also in the Neo-classical spirit.

The Ile St Louis from the
west, showing the
Pont St Louis, the quai
d'Orléans and the quai de
Béthune. The quai de
Béthune was known as the
quai des Balcons in the
eighteenth century, as a
result of Le Vau's suggestion
that all the houses bordering
the Seine on the Ile St Louis
should have exquisitely
wrought balconies.

Following pages:
236/237 Boss comprising
Greek masks at the centre of
one of the vaults in the
Grand Vestibule at Garnier's
Opera House.

Bibliography

Original dates of publication appear in brackets.

Apollinaire, Guillaume. *Le Flâneur des deux Rives*. Paris: 1928.

Architectural Design. Vol 62. London: 1992.

Architectural Review. Vol 186. London: 1989.

Aulanier, Christiane. *Histoire du palais et du musée du Louvre*. 10 vols. Paris: 1947-71.

Babelon, Jean-Pierre. *Demeures parisiennes sous Henri IV et Louis XIII*. Paris: Hazan, 1991.

Babelon, Jean-Pierre. *Le Marais, mythe et réalité*. Exhib cat. Paris: Caisse nationale des monuments historiques et des sites, 1987.

Ballon, Hilary. *The Paris of Henry IV: Architecture of Urbanism*. Cambridge, Mass: MIT Press, 1991.

de Balzac, Honoré. *La Cousine Bette*. Harmondsworth: Penguin Books, 1965 (1846).

Barozzi, Jacques. *Guide des Cimitières Parisiens*. Paris: Editions Hervas, 1990.

Baudelaire, Charles. *Les Fleurs du Mal*. London: Duckworth, 1988 (1857).

Berty, A, Legrand, H-L, and Tisserand, L-M. *Topographie Historique de vieux Paris*. Paris: 1866-97.

Blunt, Anthony. *Art and Architecture in France, 1500-1700*. Harmondsworth: Penguin Books, 1982.

Braham, Allan. *The Architecture of the French Enlightenment*. London: Thames & Hudson, 1980.

de la Bretonne, Restif. *Les nuits de Paris*. Paris: 1788.

de la Bretonne, Restif. *Vingt nuits de Paris*. Paris: 1794.

Chapman, J M, and Brian. *The Life and Times of Baron Haussmann; Paris in the Second Empire*. London: Weidenfeld & Nicolson, 1957.

Chevalier, Louis. *Montmartre – du plaisir et du crime*. Paris: Editions Robert Laffont, 1980.

Christ, Yvan. *Les Champs-Elysées, Le Faubourg Saint-Honoré*. Paris: 1982.

Christ, Yvan. *Le Faubourg Saint-Germain*. Paris: 1987.

Christ, Yvan. *Le Louvre et les Tuileries: histoire architecturale d'un double palais*. Paris: 1949.

Cochin, Charles-Nicholas. *Observations sur les antiquités de la ville d'Herculaneum*. Paris: 1757.

Contet, Frédéric. *Les Vieux Hôtels de Paris*. Paris: 1908-37.

Desgodetz, Antoine. *Les Edifices Antiques de Rome*. Rome: 1682.

Dickens, Charles. *A Tale of Two Cities*. Harmondsworth: Penguin Books, 1970 (1859).

Ducerceau, Jacques Androuet. *Les plus excellents bâtiments de France*. 2 vols. Paris: 1575-9.

Evanson, Norma. *Paris: A Century of Change, 1878-1978*. New Haven: Yale University Press, 1979.

Fournier, Edouard. *Histoire du Pont-Neuf*. 2 vols. Paris: 1862.

Fugier, A-M. *La vie élégante: formation du Tout Paris, 1815-1848*. Paris: Fayard, 1990.

Garnier, Charles. *Le Nouvel Opéra de Paris*. 2 vols. Paris: 1878-81.

von Geymüller, Heinrich. *Les Ducerceau, leur vie et leur oeuvre*. Paris: 1887.

Giesbert, Franz Olivier. *Le Président*. Paris: Seuil, 1990.

Guerrini, Maurice. *Napoleon and Paris*. London: Cassell, 1970.

Haussmann, Georges-Eugène. *Memoires du Baron Haussmann*. 2 vols. Paris: 1890-3.

Hautcoeur, Louis. *Histoire de l'Architecture Française. La Formation de l'idéal classique*. 4 vols. Paris: 1963-7.

Hazan, Fernand (ed). *Dictionnaire de Paris*. Paris: Librairie Larousse, 1964.

Hemingway, Ernest. *A Moveable Feast*. London: Macmillan, 1987 (1964).

Hillairet, Jacques. *Dictionnaire Historique des Rues de Paris*. 2 vols. Paris: Editions de Minuit, 1972.

Honour, Hugh. *Neo-classicism*. Harmondsworth: Penguin Books, 1968.

Hugo, Victor. *Les Misérables*. Harmondsworth: Penguin Books, 1982 (1862).

Hugo, Victor. *Notre Dame of Paris*. Harmondsworth: Penguin Books, 1978 (1831).

Husson, François. *Artisans français. Les serruriers. Etude historique*. 4 vols. Paris: 1902.

Krafft, J. *Portes Cochères et Portes d'Entrées de Paris*. Paris: 1810.

Laugier, M-A. *Essai sur l'architecture*. Paris: 1753.

Le Muet, Pierre. *Manière de bien bastir pour toutes sortes de personnes*. Paris: 1623 and 1647.

Le Roy, Julien David. *Les ruines des plus beaux monuments de la Grèce*. Paris, 1758.

Leroux, Gaston. *Le Fantôme de l'Opéra*. Paris: Editions Pierre Lafitte, 1922.

Lesnikowski, Wojciech. *French Avant-garde Architecture*. Chicago: Art Institute of Chicago, 1989.

Maneglier, Hervé. *Paris impérial: la vie quotidienne sous le Second Empire*. Paris: Armand Colin, 1990.

Marmontel. *Memoires de Marmontel*. English trans in *Autobiography: A collection of the most instructive and amusing lives*. Vol 2. London: 1826.

de Maupassant, Guy. *Bel-Ami*. Harmondsworth: Penguin Books, 1975 (1885).

Menestrier, C F. *Traité des tournois, joustes, carrousels, et autres spectacles publics*. Lyons: 1669.

Mondain-Monval, Jean. *Soufflot: sa vie, son oeuvre, son ésthetique (1713-1780)*. Paris: 1918.

Musée Carnavalet. *Les Grands Boulevards*. Exhib cat. Paris: Musées de la Ville de Paris, 1985.

New Paris Guide for 1851. Paris: Galignani, 1851.

Nuitter, C. *Le Nouvel Opéra de Paris*. Paris: 1875.

l'Orme, Philibert de. *Architecture*. Paris: 1648.

Ory, Pascal. *Les Expositions Universelles de Paris*. Paris: Ramsay Image, 1982.

Pinçon, M, and Pinçon-Charlot, M. *Dans les Beaux Quartiers*. Paris: Seuil, 1989.

Pinkney, David H. *Napoleon III and the re-building of Paris*. New Jersey: Princeton University Press, 1958.

Proust, Marcel. *A La Recherche du Temps Perdu*. Harmondsworth: Penguin Books, 1983 (1913-27).

Rabelais, François. *Gargantua and Pantagruel*. Harmondsworth: Penguin Books, 1955 (1534).

Rigaud, André. *Paris: ses rues et ses fantômes*. Paris: Editions Berger-Levrault, 1972.

Rousset-Charny, Gérard. *Les palais parisiens de la belle epoque*. Paris: Délégation à l'action artistique de la Ville de Paris, 1990.

Sand, George. *Oeuvres autobiographiques*. 2 vols. Paris: Gallimard, 1970.

Say, Léon. *Le Chemin de Fer. Guide par les principaux écrivains et artists de la France*. 2 vols. Paris: 1867.

de Sevigné, Madame. *Les Lettres*. Paris: 1640-96.

Thierry, L-V. *Guide des amateurs et des étrangers voyeurs à Paris*. Paris: 1787.

Viollet-le-Duc, Eugène-Emanuel. *Dictionnaire raisonnée de l'architecture française*. Paris: 1858-68.

Viollet-le-Duc, Eugène-Emanuel. *Entretiens sur l'architecture*. 2 vols. Paris: 1863 and 1872.

Voltaire. *Oeuvres Complètes*. Paris: 1776-8.

Voltaire. *Le Siècle de Louis XIV*. Paris: 1756.

Zeldin, Theodore. *The French*. London: HarperCollins, 1983.

Zola, Emile. *L'Assommoir*. Harmondsworth: Penguin Books, 1970 (1887).

Zola, Emile. *Nana*. Harmondsworth: Penguin Books, 1972 (1880).

Zola, Emile. *Paris*. Crayford: Gordon Press, 1981 (1889).

Index